Ballet Mad

A Ballet Fan
Remembers

Ballet Mad

A Ballet Fan
Remembers

STEPHANIE BATT

NONSUCH

First published 2006

Nonsuch Publishing Limited
73 Lower Leeson Street
Dublin 2
Ireland
www.nonsuch-publishing.com

British Library Cataloguing in Publication Data.
A catalogue record for this book is available from the British Library.

ISBN 1 84588 548 1

Typesetting and origination by Tempus Publishing Limited.
Printed in Great Britain.

Contents

Acknowledgements

I would like to acknowledge the help and support of my family, especially my three girls, Karina, Ciara and Aoife. Their technical expertise was invaluable. Two current ballet aficionados, Mary Dundon and Una Walsh, have helped with information and insights into the world of ballet. As dancers, they have made very helpful observations. I am indebted to Monica Loughman who has kindly written the Foreword and was very encouraging and supportive. My Publisher, Eoin Purcell of Nonsuch, has been extremely patient with a first-time author, my thanks to him. Finally to my long-time friend and technical adviser, Noirin Scully, my heartfelt thanks. It is a cliché, but without her help, this book would never have got past the notebook stage!

Foreword

Having spent more than half my life in Russia training hard to become a Ballerina and then working full-time as a professional ballet dancer, I find that my best means of communication is on the stage and not the printed word. So, bear with me!

Before my company, The Tchaikovsky Perm State Ballet of Russia, ever performed in the Point Theatre we performed briefly in Dublin's Olympia Theatre. Back then, I couldn't help but feel that we were performing on such an inadequate stage. We were used to the theatre in Perm, which has a stage about three times the size of the Oympia's. So our main concerns were that we would crash into each other in the wings, bump into each other while dancing and perhaps even run out of room during a variation. A lot of the Russian's expressed their concern and I remember that our Artistic Director gave me a particularly cold stare of disbelief when he saw the size of the stage. I couldn't help but feel ashamed. Little did I know then that the Olympia Theatre had hosted the most prestigious ballet companies in the world. Some of the most prolific ballet dancers ever have performed on the Olympia's stage. I can't help but wish that this book had been available to show my colleagues (and the Artistic Director) that Ireland too has a wealthy ballet history.

This book is a factual, informative and an excellent read for the balletomane. It provides incredible historical insight into ballet in Ireland.

Monica Loughman
27 August 2005

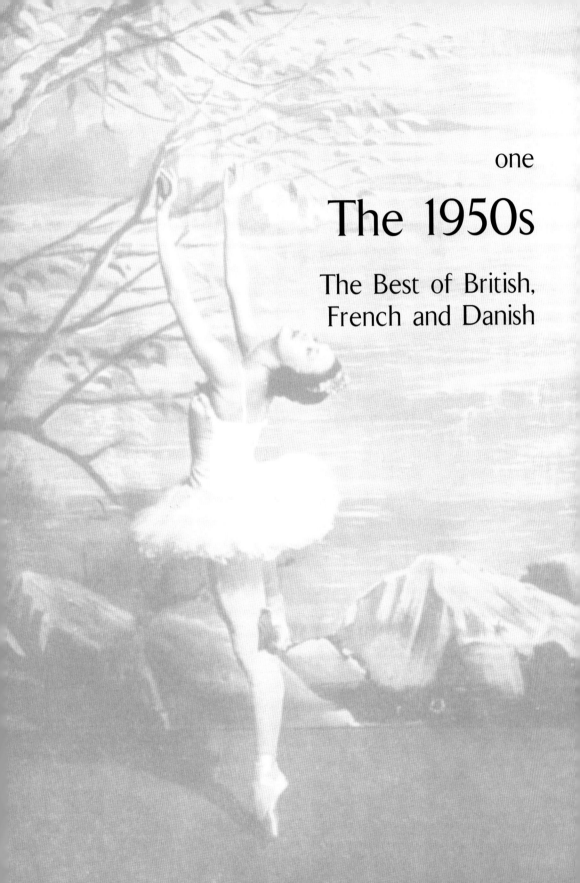

one

The 1950s

The Best of British, French and Danish

Left: Stephanie Kenna in her younger days

Opposite left: Reproduction of drawn figures

Opposite right: Anna Pavlova

From the very first time I attended a ballet performance in Dublin's Gaiety Theatre I was completely hooked.

But my interest had been whetted at an early age by local presentations by Miss Catt's and Miss Tully's ballet schools in which friends and a neighbour, Toni O'Farrell, featured. I longed to do likewise.

As a hockey-playing schoolgirl, whose maturing contours and proportions precluded a serious career in ballet, and being a late starter, I ignored that sad but obvious fact and felt that inside my sturdy frame there was a svelte creature just waiting to emerge, and that years of dedication and practice would eventually fit me, at least, for the corps de ballet.

My parents, who could ill afford to do so, indulged this somewhat latent desire (on the flimsy evidence of my dancing a solo as Winter in the school's very first production) and allowed me to attend classes with teacher Annette Hynes. I thoroughly enjoyed and benefited from these but it became painfully apparent that, hampered by a certain lack of equilibrium, I would be better off concentrating on participation in the school's hockey team. Progression to expensive blocked shoes reinforced this view. This was a decision, though not taken without regret, which has given me so many years of enjoyment in the comradeship of team sport in the course of a long and undistinguished 'career' in hockey.

The requirements for a future dancer are that she/he should have good deportment, correct physical proportions, and certain attributes such as a long neck and not-too-

broad shoulders combined with finely and not too heavily muscled legs, slender hips and under-average *avoir du poids*. Upon this can be built good *port de bras*; placement; epaulement and the gradual, very gradual programme of exercises that are the 'tools' of a dancer's trade. And that is just the physical side! One requires an innate musicality, a sense of theatricality and a subjection to stage and classroom discipline.

I continued with practice however, for a while, and my life-long enthusiasm for classical ballet in particular has remained with me.

At around this time I read about Joan Denise Moriarty and her school in Cork in an article in the *Junior Digest* – an Irish publication that came out monthly. The photograph showed Betty Long and Milo Lynch being taught at the barre by Joan Denise Moriarty. Also in this *Digest* in a later issue there was an article about Anna Pavlova, which was so exciting and different. A weekly comic for teenage girls called *GIRL* ran a serial called 'Belle of the Ballet' featuring a blonde Russian waif. Like many another, I eagerly awaited Wednesdays when my copy (on order) was read and reread and the 'exercises' scrutinised.

Another great influence was Noel Streatfield's book *Ballet Shoes* – a fascinating story. The local Carnegie Library in Dun Laoghaire was a wonderful source of information. Each book on the subject was taken out. Many times I was tempted to remove photos of ballerinas, or scenes from the ballet. By now I was making thrice-weekly visits and taking home heavy tomes of musical 'scores' with which I struggled in frustration at the difficult keys.

The book I borrowed most often was a sort of pictorial dictionary of steps and exercises by Kay Ambrose. I drew literally hundreds of little figures myself, and practiced constantly at the barre in front of a full-length mirror in my practice dress. I enjoyed the delusion of dressing in my tutu and gathering my long thick hair into a classical chignon and hairnet, and wearing a 'swan' headdress.

The walls of my room were covered with pictures from *GIRL* of famous dancers: Margot Fonteyn, Moira Shearer, Beryl Grey, Diaghilev's Baby Ballerinas and Alicia Markova, and those virile male *danseurs*: Nijinsky, the legendary Russian dancer and partner of Tamara Karsavina, Fokine, dancer and choreographer, Massine, Anton Dolin, the Russian trained Anglo-Irish dancer who would delight us all in Dublin in the future.

I knew that there had been ballet performances in Dublin before my first experience of a professional company in 1952, but on that day I became not just a crazed would-be dancer, but a balletomane – a title invented by Arnold Haskell, that well-known writer of many books on the Dance.

I had read of visiting companies to Cork and Dublin. Stanley Judson, who had danced with Pavlova, undertook what turned out to be an ill-fated tour, which was denounced by local clergy in Cork as being immodest. They had to wire to London for money to take them home. Cepta Cullen's production of *Les Papillons* was given in the Capitol in Dublin in 1943 and indeed Pavlova herself appeared in the Theatre Royal, in 1930 I think it was. The Sadlers Wells Ballet appeared at the Gaiety in 1938, no doubt encouraged by Ninette de Valois (Edris Stannus of Baltinglass).

There were probably other stalwarts promoting ballet in Ireland, but for me it all started on 14 June 1952 with a performance of *Swan Lake* danced by Mona Inglesby's International Ballet Company. The Company had appeared in 1950, before I was permitted to go to the theatre. I was simply overwhelmed, both by the beauty of Mona Inglesby, the drama of the White Act, the Court Act and the final 'tragic' ending to the wonderful Tchaikovsky score, and couldn't wait to go again the following Wednesday to see *The Sleeping Princess* (originally known as *The Sleeping Beauty*). This time the Princess was danced by Claudie Algeranova, Algeranoff was Carabosse, Helene Armfelt was the Lilac Fairy and Vladimir Kalishkevsky was the Prince. Oh, the wonder of it all! Two wonderful Tchaikovsky ballets to start me off, could one ask for more?

I'd been given a tiny autograph book for Christmas and now, interspersed with treasured entries by school pals' verses, were the names of the Stars of the International Ballet Company. The Stage-Door Syndrome had commenced.

As far as I can recall, this was a three-week season – quite a risk for a ballet company back in the '50s. It must have been worth it, because the company returned in July 1953 for another two weeks, giving a programme similar to 1950, of *Visions*, an award-winning ballet choreographed by Julian Algo to a Mousskorsky score; *Endymion*, by Mona Inglesby (costumes by Sophie Fedorovitch) and *Gaieté Parisienne* which brought the roof down! Mona Inglesby danced the Glove Seller. In my diary I noted twelve curtain calls! I had got tickets for these performances and went with a school pal, Ann O'Donnell. Neither of us knew anything much about full- length ballets but we were aware that the Seniors (i.e. Leaving Cert class) like Mary Cogan, Evelyn Francis, her sister Moya and Patricia Boylan were already aficionados. We felt very grown up, 'discussing' the performance with them the next day!

The programme had opened with *Les Sylphides*. Always a Chopin fan, having listened to my mother playing waltzes, mazurkas, preludes and nocturnes on the piano, I was enthralled from the curtain up. How I now envy anyone seeing their first *Sylphides* and how I wish I could re-live those magical moments. I particularly remember the exquisite dancing of June Summers, in a cast that included Herida May, Joyce Gearing, Bridget Kelly and Harvey Krefets. I was still in a daze for the first half of *Visions*, which followed.

Coppelia was my third Big Ballet. Inglesby again starred, and again, it was all pure magic, receiving thirteen curtain calls from an enthusiastic audience, as it was the last night of the season. I had never experienced anything quite like it. Miss Inglesby, who had started the company herself during wartime in England, made a speech thanking Dublin audiences for their warm reception. Bouquets were presented to the female principals. I was simply mesmerised. I had never witnessed anything like this although I knew that flowers were delivered to dressing rooms. Later I heard that there were professional 'flower throwers' in certain large theatres in England and many years later, experienced the ordinary fan in Russia hurling flowers from the side boxes onto the stage. The whole evening was so exciting and glamorous that we didn't want it to end.

At the time, we were able to secure tickets locally in Dun Laoghaire at a ticket agency, but on this Last Night we had decided to queue for the 'Gods'. The 'Gods' was the topmost Gallery, which was unreserved, so-called because it was so near to Heaven! Seating was rudimentary wooden 'benches' and applause was demonstrated by stamping our feet. We went in early and were stationed in the queue at the Stage Door area for hours. As we were so well placed, we saw arrivals and got early autographs and some of us even got coveted shoes. I got one from Sophia Trant, and when Mona Inglesby arrived (by taxi) I asked her for one, greatly daring. She promised she would keep me one and after the performance we rushed down to the Stage Door again and waited for ages. Various soloists came out and threw shoes to us (my friend got one) but when Mona Inglesby appeared she only had one pair, signed across the toe, and she gave one TO ME! Oh, the joy! Talk about floating home……..
Actually, we had to run at top speed, as the 46A was the only bus we could both safely get at that hour and we didn't want to miss it. We had no taxi money!

In fact we had very little money for any activity. Walking or cycling, not bussing, was our usual mode of transport. Taxis would have been unheard of. In the first years of Senior School we all wore lisle stockings, but in later years we wore nylon (stockings), which laddered easily and one's parents only provided a certain number of pairs per term. One could mend them oneself or pay to have them invisibly mended. It was considered 'infra dig' to revert to lisle stockings except for Games or in extremely cold weather, when there was the distinct possibility of getting chilblains. Paying to have nylons mended cost money we could ill afford, so we learnt to be very careful, and to stop potential runs with clear nail polish!

Of course ballet leotards and tights were very expensive but did not wear out as quickly as *pointe* shoes. We realised that a principal dancer could use up to as many as three pairs in a long ballet, but dancers too, were relatively poorly paid and had to economise in other ways. In the 40s and 50s dancers had their silk tights repaired time and time again, or indeed repaired them themselves using little hooks! This is information is supplied by Margot Fonteyn, in her autobiography. She also points out that ballet shoemakers were permitted the necessary materials in wartime, to carry out their work.

After World War Two living was relatively simple. The average middleclass family may have had a car, but petrol was rationed during the war and an expensive commodity afterwards. Clothes were often handed down, altered or 'turned' and everyone considered this normal. Exotic extras, such as horse riding or ballet lessons were beyond the pockets of most parents, who very often had families of five or six children. Thus the extra curricular activities provided in the secondary schools were a wonderful outlet and in winter and summer, a variety of sports and athletics were

Photograph of school friends in 1954. From left to right, back row: Michelle Costelloe, Clodagh Power, Emer Cullen. Middle row: Claire Fenlon, Ann O'Donnell, Rosemary Boothmen. Front row: Stephanie Kenna and Valerie Little

catered for. We took it for granted at the time, but in reality we realised we were the lucky ones. For a small student bus fare outlay we had visits to other schools for weekend matches and competitions. Many were not so fortunate.

I was a day border at Loreto Foxrock with just one uniform 'tunic', woollen sweater and several blouses worn with a tie. This was before the days of sports wear, and our uniform was worn for every activity from classroom to hockey-pitch to drill and marching.

But back to the ballet!

'J.J.F' gave a review of the 1953 International season – my first newspaper 'cutting'- describing Mona Inglesby's performance, partnered by Ernest Hewitt in the *Sleeping Beauty* (Princess).

INTERNATIONAL BALLET OPENS GAIETY SEASON

★ INTERNATIONAL BALLET is the one company that contrives to make the Gaiety stage look smaller that it actually is.

International is, of course, a large company, but not altogether that much greater than others that have appeared on the same stage.

Perhaps the explanation for this recurring optical illusion is that the members of International spread themselves more than their rivals, that they demand, per person, more dancing space.

Whatever the reason, one wished last evening, especially during the opening act, that the dancing area, large though it undoubtedly was, could be larger still, and that the side draperies could be hung further back. But if that were and could be done, people in side seats might complain that they were missing some of the dancing.

★

The ballet seen was the full-length and glittering "Sleeping Beauty." There were new sets, first seen during the company's recent season in Barcelona.

Tchaikovsky's music, although not as continually attractive as that for "Swan Lake," is beguiling. Some of Petipa's dance patterns now seem rather stereotyped, certainly the parade of nursery tale characters in the final act has been copied, and surpassed, elsewhere in the theatrical field.

The role of Princess Aurora, however, remains one of the major parts in ballet, demanding for its proper portrayal the highest technique equipment and great purity of line.

The necessary qualities were present in Mona Inglesby's performance, which had a star's sparkle. The control of movement was brilliantly achieved, especially in the

Mona Inglesby

famous "Rose" dance in the second act.

Ernest Hewitt has happily recovered from the leg injury that kept him out of a production of "Swan Lake" in Manchester last week. The role of the Prince is unexacting from a dancing point of view. Hewitt gave an excellent acting performance.

Algeranoff out a suitably sinister figure as Carabosse the wicked fairy, and Herida May made a splendid Lilac Fairy. Robert Emblen got an ovation for his dancing as the Bluebird in the final act.

The dancing of the other members of the company showed fine attack. The orchestra was conducted by James Walker.

J. J. F.

DANNY CUMMINS BACK IN TOWN

★ DANNY CUMMINS, back after his tour with the

He acclaims her Rose Adagio, and Herida May's Lilac Fairy as well as Ronald Emblen's Bluebird. Domini Callaghan also appeared. There was another favourable review by 'B.Q' of Mona Inglesby as Coppélia, but yet another describes her Glove Seller as being of 'English Miss' wholesomeness. I didn't agree with this, nor did Carolyn Swift, but it may well be that her English background did come through. A very determined lady, she had worked as an ambulance driver during the war in London, and even during that time of raids and bombing she gathered a corps of dancers together and founded her company, which made its first appearance at the Alhambra Theatre, Glasgow in 1941. She did indeed have 'international' dancers, Stanislas Idikowsky was *maitre de ballet*, Nina Tarakanova and Harold Turner and she herself were principals, later augmented by several other 'foreign' dancers. She was also a choreographer (Amoras, Endymion and Everyman). She had danced with the Ballets Rambert and with the Dandré Russian Ballet at Covent Garden. It was a very courageous step for quite a young woman to assemble her own company in mid-wartime at a time when the Ballets Rambert and Sadler's Wells ballet were also struggling to maintain production – and audiences. Dublin was fortunate that she and her company travelled to our shores.

On turning over the review page of the newspaper in 1953 I came across headlines of news items such as: 'Call- up of all men up to age 40 to the Cambodian army' and 'Kenya must have more Police to ensure the 'end' of the MauMau', ' Twenty-one people died on one day of sunstroke in Peshawar, Pakinstan.' The International Ballet came to Dublin again the next year, but I was not able to go to see them. Sadly, I never saw them again.

Above left and right: Programme photos of Belinda Wright and John Gilpin

ANTON DOLIN

Left: Programme photo of Anton Dolin

Above: Sonia Arova

But my enthusiasm never wore off, and in February 1953 the next Company came to Dublin. It was 'Festival Ballet', Artistic Director/Danseur Noble: Anton Dolin (Patrick Healy-Kaye). Here was 'one of our own', as he had an Irish grandmother! He had studied and danced with the greats and was already well known. However I wasn't to see him dance during this first week and it was the utterly delectable Belinda Wright, partnered by the altogether amazing John Gilpin in *Harliquinade* (choreography Darnell, music Drigo) which totally captivated me. I was availing of my mother's seat, as she was ill, and was sitting with her knowledgeable friend. I was close to the stage for the first time and was able to see the expressive mime, as well as the intricacies of the steely pointe work of Wright. This was followed by *Casse-Noisette* (*Nutcracker*) (Dolin and Beriosoff, after Ivanov), as enchanting a ballet as one could wish to see, with Sonia Arova, John Gilpin and Belinda Wright. There were twelve rapturous curtain calls at the conclusion of the ballet. I have seen it so many times since and none had surpassed the magic of this first performance.

Festival Ballet was founded in 1950, named for the Festival of Britain. In 1930 Anton Dolin had danced with Ninette de Valois. He and Alicia Markova had both danced with Diaghilev and subsequently had had a very successful partnership in London and U.S. and indeed elsewhere in Europe. They had formed a company pre-war and now the new company embarked on its own course, having headquarters at the Festival Hall. However, Markova had departed the company in 1952. Dolin had a fascinating career in ballet and in show business and had a network of international contacts in ballet, film and theatre. His professional partnership with Markova is legendary but he was never merely the noble partner but a dancer and personality in his own right. His Anglo-Irish background gave him confidence and charm and a great adaptability. His direction was paramount in the new Company, but not as 'star of the show'. He encouraged his young company, while dancing some roles himself – nonetheless imbuing them with star quality.

I noted the prices given in the programme (not given for the International). Box Seats were 12/6, Dress Circle 12/6, 10/6, parterre 10/6, 7/6; Upper Circle 5/- and Gallery 2/-. This of course, was old money, prior to decimalisation and the euro, when 10/6d equalled roughly 1 euro.

A selection of advertisements were shown on the Safety Curtain and the programmes had advertisements such as: The Brendan Smith Academy of Acting; Whelans for Dancing; W.R. Duncan for Furs and Johnston Mooney & O'Brien for Bread. Dunn's of D'Olier St. for Fish; Boyers Dept. Store; Tylers (of course) for Shoes featured, as did The Subway Restaurant; Hely's Sports Equipment; The Tower Bar (men only served); Cafollas of Ice Cream fame; May's for Records; Thwaites for soda water; Lucky Cody for Sweep tickets, and Joe Douglas for Bouquets – many of which were fashioned as offerings to the Principal Dancers and Orchestral

A Romantic Ballet

★ Anton Dolin made one of his now regrettably infrequent performances in a long Ballet in 'Giselle' at the **Gaiety** last night.

His Alberecht in this venerable work which holds the essence of German romanticism, had a splendid all-over sense of style and his lightness on his feet was something to applaud, which the audience did in no uncertain manner

Natalie Krassovska mimed beautifully the innocent village maid of the first act, and brought a strikingly remote quality to her portrayal in the second act of the spirit of Giselle.

The second act was by far the better; in it the concerted movements had greater smoothness, and absent were the rough edges of some of the patterns by the corps de ballet in the first act. Janet Overton was an ethereal Queen of the Wilis.

The enthusiasm of the audience at the end of the performance was unbounded

John Gilpin and Belinda Wright were delightfully gay and frivolous in an extract from "Harlequinade."

The evening was brought to a close with a further performance of " Symphony for Fun."

J. J. F.

Small newspaper review of *Giselle*

Natalie Krassovska

Conductors- James Walker and Anthony Baines (International) and Geoffrey Corbett (Festival) who each conducted their respective orchestras.

These two-week seasons gave us a real chance to get to know the dancers, principals, soloists and corps alike. Alas, this does not happen nowadays, when a season may last a mere three days. I was fortunate to have made six trips to the Gaiety, taken by various family benefactors, including my aunts Cora and Madge and 'sponsored' by my Godmother Aunt Maureen and treated by my parents, ~~my parents, Kevin and Trassa Kenna. My aunt Geraldine paid the subscription~~ to the Dance magazines that I so enjoyed. I shall always be so grateful to all of them.

During that 1953 season *Concerto Grosso* (Lichine, Vivaldi) was the first pure ballet of this kind that I'd seen and I revelled in the sheer classicism of it. A true 'classic' followed with *Giselle* danced by Nathalie Leslie (Krassovska) and Anton Dolin. He had already danced in *Vision of Marguerite*, but this was a very special occasion indeed, as everyone realised. (Choreography: Dolin after Corelli). When I'd recovered from the tragedy and mystique of all, I rushed to the the Dun Laoghaire Library to get the Adam score. Many say it is a trite score, but it suits the romanticism of the

Newspaper photo of Green Table when it was performed in the Olympia, Dublin

choreography. *Symphony for Fun* completed this long programme, ending it on a light 'fun' note, after which I noted that there were fourteen curtain calls.

The second week also presented Act 2 of *Swan Lake*, *Spectre de la Rose* danced by John Gilpin and Belinda Wright – later he was to dance it with Dame Margot Fonteyn. Tamara Karsavina helped Dolin to reproduce this Weber ballet, made famous by herself and Nijinsky. Another famous vignette *Pas de Quatre* with Krassovska, Sonia Arova, Wright and Noel Rosanna taking the parts created by Cerrito, Grahn, Taglioni and Elssler. Act 2 of the *Nutcracker* danced by Krassovska and Oleg Briansky ended a varied and splendid evening, with eleven curtain calls. I attended this performance with Claire Fenlon, another school pal and made great use of her binoculars!

Surely the International and Festival Companies were bringing ballet to Dublin, much as Joan Denise Moriarty and John Regan of Limerick were bringing the dance to smaller towns in Ireland. We have reason to be grateful to all the Directors for presenting so much variety and for developing our taste and appreciation for the ballet. Some Irish-sounding names appeared in the programmes- Michael Hogan was a dashing soloist with Festival Ballet and Bridget Kelly danced with the International Ballet, as did Domini Callaghan.

Photo of recent Ballet Ireland version of *Alice* from the *Irish Times*

We Irish have always loved dancing as can be witnessed from our literature and even mythology and we are open to enjoy all types of Dance. Our own tradition includes sean-nós dancing, set-dancing, céile dancing and 'pure' Irish dancing. All are quite different and some quite skilful, differing greatly in technique from ballet, modern or indeed Spanish.

The visiting Spanish companies enjoyed, if that is the correct word, some of the most tumultuous receptions given in the capital. Pilar Lopez and her Company visited Dublin three times, Luisillo and Jose Greco in 1956 to name a few, had us clapping and cheering at the Olympia— the zapateado held us spellbound. The true Flamenco of the singers, guitars and dancers touched a chord in the Irish soul – later to surface in the tremendous reception given to *Riverdance* when it was presented as the interval entertainment on the occasion of Ireland hosting the European Song Contest.

Also at the Olympia, the Ballets Joos presented *Song of Youth* (Handel), *The Big City* and *Le Bosquet*. But the *pièce de resistance* was the anti-war ballet *The Green Table*. The Olympia's programmes featured Piggots, the musical instruments specialists, Lenehans hardware; both Odearest and Hiltonia mattresses; Gings; Hector Grey; The Singing Kettle, and McCabes Bar & Lounge. Also featured was McCabes Fish & Poultry. No seat prices were given but programmes were 6d.

1954 was a very special year. Festival Ballet came in March with new soloists dancing *Les Sylpides* – Marilyn Burr Daphne Dale as well as Krassovska and Nicholai Polajenko. *Alice in Wonderland*, (recently mounted in 2005 Cork and in Dublin at several venues by Ballet Ireland). This ballet (choreography Michael Charnley; music Horovitz) was one close to Dolin's heart and he spoke the narration – a novelty for me. Belinda Wright was perfect as Alice and who else but Gilpin as the White Rabbit? The cast was of a high standard and we had got to know and recognise most of the dancers, being super-critical of new members. I recorded six curtain calls after this new ballet and ten after the programme of the evening ended. *Le Beau Danube* to Johann Strauss music was delightful, thoroughly enjoyed by dancers and audience alike and featuring the soloists as 'Stars'. These were now the signatories in my autograph book, which now included Dolin, Gilpin, Krassovska and Wright, Sonia Arova, Polajenko, Briansky, Emblen, Jeannette Minty, Peter White, Wolfgang Brunner and the irrepressible Keith Beckett. There was also the lovely Janet Overton, Diane Richards, Pamela Hart, Russell Kerr, et al – all of whom patiently and graciously signed our books and programmes.

Boxes had gone up to £5, £3/15, £2/10 and Dress Circle 12/6, Parterre 10/-, Upper Circle 5/- and The Gods remained at 2/- - Thank God – as we wanted to go to as many performances as possible. We no longer booked and raced in early after school, or, on Saturdays, after a hockey match, relieving whomsoever we could inveigle to stand in the queue for us until we arrived. Thereafter we would relieve each other and dash over to Robert Roberts for beans on toast, or just toast and tea! Although it was often very cold, I don't remember actually queuing in the rain.

My second *Nutcracker* was as enjoyable as ever, if lacking that first magical impact, and had Krassovska in the *Grand Pas*, and Anita Landa and Louis Godfrey in the *Danse Espagnol*. For me the highlight of this week's programme was the hypnotic dancing to the equally hypnotic music of Ravel, of Anton Dolin in the famous *Bolero*. I'm sure his prime dancing days were behind him, but he gave a spellbinding and never-to-be-forgotten performance. *Prince Igor* – some of the music of which was so familiar to us because of the musical *Kismet*, was last of the night's entertainment. Daphne Dale danced the captive Persian Princess. Fokine's choreography, reproduced by Nicolai Beriosoff to Borodin's exciting music, was a real treat and ended the first weeks' programme.

Act One of *Swan Lake*, with Belinda Wright and John Gilpin; the *pas de quatre* and the Black Swan *pas de deux* were the first offerings of the new week and Krassovska was in fine and flashing form with the famous thirty-two *fouettés* becoming sixty-four as she gave an encore. So many of the great ballerinas find this tour de force a tremendous challenge, others do not. Apparently the Italians first 'misstressed' them (Legnani was the first to achieve thirty-two) and passed the secret on to Nicholas Legat, who observed and then trained the Russian Ballerinas in this exacting technique (the first being Mathilde Kschessinskya). Nureyev, too, had a tip for Dame Margot who had found them difficult up to that point.

Old photograph of Marie Rambert

Vilia was an *operette dansee* and got a mixed and vociferous reception. I enjoyed it thoroughly. Dolin was dancing The Baron and Daphne Dale The Widow to Franz Lehar music (choreography Ruth Page). There was some booing and I suppose one could say critical acclaim but it received fifteen curtain calls. 'We want Gilpin' called the Gods, and he did appear on stage – in street clothes. 'We want Dolin', we cried and he literally sprang onto the stage and made a speech. Festival Ballet was not to reappear for two years.

I list as many ballet as possible, also dancers, to give readers an idea of the vast number of ballets mounted, which must have been so expensive, and of the diversity between the classics and modern ballets. What a debt we owe to these two companies alone.

Also in September 1954 the Ballets Rambert paid us a visit, once again to the Gaiety. Marie Rambert, 'Mim' (Miryam Ramberg) who had studied in her native Poland, and in Russia, held auditions in Dublin. She had also been closely associated with Nijinsky and understood his revolutionary choreography and how it should be interpreted. Again, it was a two -week season and her dancers included Mary Munro, Alexander Bennett, Beryl Goldwyn, Noreen Sopwith, Anne Lascelles, Norman Dixon, Anne Horn and Terry Gilbert. Of course, they were new to us, although those of us who subscribed to *The Dancing Times* or *Dance and Dancers* were familiar with some of the names.

Pierina Legnani

They also presented *Les Sylphides*, *Swan Lake* Act Two and *Giselle*. In addition, there was *Façade* (choreography Frederick Ashton, music William Walton) reproduced in the original version, known only to me from photographs. A delight! *Gala Performance* (Prokofiev/Anthony Tudor) to me was delightful too. Three different 'Schools' of ballet were given an interpretation by 'Russian', 'French and 'Italian' ballerinas. Others find it too lightweight. I adored it – exaggerated mannerisms and all. Noreen Sopwith was outstanding. Mme. Rambert made a long speech on the opening night, and was well received. On the last night Alexander Bennett gave the speech, thanking the audience on behalf of Mme. Rambert. Walter Gore's *Winter Night* to Rachmaninoff's second piano concerto was the highlight of the season for me – the sad tale of the New Love supplanting the Old.

Dublin Applauds Alicia Markova

YESTERDAY afternoon the Theatre Royal audience thundered its applause at the first Dublin appearance of Alicia Markova, the world-famous English ballerina. Her lightness, precision and superb phrasing immediately convinced the hundreds present who had never seen her before that she is indeed the brilliant classical dancer that authorities and public opinion alike long ago claimed.

Dance recital is, in my opinion, a very poor substitute for a full-scale ballet programme, particularly in the case of the suite of dances from "Les Sylphides," a ballet which depends so much on the work of the corps to give full effect to Fokine's choreography; but, as an expedient enabling us to see a great dancer we might otherwise miss, we can only be grateful and accept it without carping. Indeed, the black velvet curtain backing used throughout was infinitely preferable to anything less than ideal decor, and enhanced the effect of the traditional black-and-white "Sylphides" costumes.

Milorad Miskovitch proved to be a reliable and finished partner in classical work and a fine dancer in his own right. In Nijinsky's controversial "L'Apres-Midi d'un Faune," which caused a sensation on its first presentation by Diaghileff in Paris, he gave an unforgettable performance.

Although Markova gave a moving performance of Pavlova's famous "Dying Swan" (with choreography by Fokine to Saint Saens's music), and her exceptional lightness showed to great effect in the Chopin suite, I preferred her in "Bolero 1830" and the grand pas-de-deux from the Petipa-Ivanov "Nutcracker Suite," her style seeming to me more suited to classical than romantic ballet, but the Theatre Royal audience undoubtedly chose "The Dying Swan," forcing her to take curtain after curtain.

The dancers were expertly accompanied on two pianos by Liza Fuchsova and David Tidboald, who also opened the programme by playing Chopin's "Polonaise in A," and Liza Fuchsova completed the programme with a number of piano solos. Her technical brilliance is well suited to the virtuosity of Liszt's "Venezia e Napoli," but is never allowed to diminish her playing of Saint Saens, Chopin and Debussy to mere technique.

CAROLYN SWIFT.

Feather-light ballerina Alicia Markova and Milorad Miskovitch dance to the music of Chopin at the Theatre Royal yesterday.

Photo of Markova and Miskovitch

We were now getting used to the new faces, from viewing on-stage to waiting at the stage door to see them in civvies! *Love Knots* and *Death and the Maiden* were the other two new ballets and I'm afraid they made no lasting impression on me. I was in heaven when given a shoe by Beryl Goldwyn, whom I particularly admired. I loved her in *Giselle*, and in fact loved this whole production. It seemed to me to be the most natural one – no stars as such. Anthony Tudor's *Lilac Garden* a modern classic (music Chausson) was a ballet I'd wanted to see and I wasn't disappointed. It was another melancholy story of disappointed love. Less interesting, though rousing, was the *Life and Death of Lola Montez*, featuring Audrey Nichols whom I'd seen as the French dancer in *Gala Performance*. *Peter and the Wolf* went down well – I recorded seven curtain calls – but I don't have a very clear recollection of it.

There were already four weeks of balletic variety in 1954 but it was in May of that year that an International Star came to Ireland. It was Alice Marks, whose mother was a Barry from Cork. She had studied in London and had danced with Diaghilev as Alicia Markova. She was now famous for her partnership with Anton Dolin and of course was a well-known ballerina in her own right. She was one of the smallest, most exquisitely light of ballerinas; she had made several famous roles her own at the Vic Wells, in the U.S. and at Festival Ballet and was now dancing recitals all over the world.

By great good fortune we managed to get seats for this once-off performance in the vast Theatre Royal. This was the third theatre built on the site, and was reputed to have held about 3,000 patrons. The excitement was intense. We were so high up that we needed our opera glasses (borrowed from my godmother) to see the tiny figure as she danced the Nocturne, Mazurka, Prelude and Valse from *Les Sylphides* partnered by Milorad Miskovitch. How can I describe such lightness and effortlessness? I can't. It was pure magic. I could hardly have imagined her dancing with such fire in *Bolero*, since most roles associated with her are classical in the extreme. But in this and in *L'Après Midi d'un Faune* which followed, there was a complete contrast, showing two other sides to her artistry – difficult to achieve in the Royal, with just back- drops. She revived the ballet to coincide with the 25th Anniversary of the death of Diaghilev.

The Dying Swan was of course memorable, as was the *Grand Pas* from the *Nutcracker*, danced with great élan and authority, which completed the programme given by this legendary artiste. We were privileged to see her dance and subsequently to obtain her autograph. Dame Alicia Markova died in December 2004.

1954 must have been a landmark year in what I call the Golden Age of Ballet in Dublin, as distinct from Cork, which was progressing its own important path of producing ballet in Ireland. In fact, Dame Ninette de Valois, Dame Marie Rambert and Dame Alicia Markova were patrons of the Ballet in Cork, both amateur and professional.

After the Festival Ballet and Markova's visit and before the Ballets Rambert in September we had a first visit from Les Ballets de France de Janine Charrat in June 1954 for one week at the Olympia. So it can be seen that the ballet was an important part of the cultural life of the capital with a large and faithful audience.

French dancers, such as Janine Charrat and Helene Trailine headed a talented company, known only through the pages of the *Dancing Times*. The style of dancing seemed to be very different, as could be seen when they danced, for instance, *Pas de Quatre*. Helene Trailine was magnificent and malevolent as the Black Swan and Janine Charrat was superb in the *Concierto de Grieg* to her own choreography. *Entre deux Rondes* was new to me as was *Herakles*. Neither ballet has imprinted itself on my memory but the dancing was crisp and dramatic as it was also in *Le Massacre des Amazons*.

Readers will appreciate just what a vintage year 1954 was in Dublin. The dancers were also unknown to me, Maria Fris, Vladimir Oukhtomsky, Esteban Cerda and guest artist Jean Guelis, who did not dance as he strained a ligament. Peter van Dijk and Maris Fris were dancers from Germany.

Janine Charrat paid Dublin a return visit in 1955 to the Olympia. Queuing for the Gods there was even more fraught. The street was narrow, cold and breezy. You had to get there even earlier. I had the impression that the Gods there weren't as accommodating as at the Gaiety, but I may be wrong. They seemed to be nearer to the stage.

Above: Newspaper photo of Janine Charrat and Peter van Dijk

Left: Anna Pavlova Remembered

In memory of Anna Pavlova

THE all-star festival of French ballet opened its second programme at Olympia last night with the Lifar-Lalo *Suite an Blanc,* most acceptably danced by Janine Charrat's company.

Outstanding items were the *pas de trois* by Helen Trailine, Jean Bernard Lemoine and Milko Sparemblek; Jean Bernard Lemoine's Mazurke; Ethery Pagava's contributions of *La Cigarette* and *La Flute;* and the *pas de deux* danced by Janine Monin and Milko Sparemblek.

Nor must we forget the good team-work of the supporting company.

Ludmilla Tcherina again danced *Le Cygne* in memory of Pavlova; it will be interesting to compare this performance with Janine Charrat's (which I missed on her last visit) when she dances it for the first three nights of next week.

Old legend

La Dryade, based on an old romantic legend to music by Jordania, after Adolphe Adam, was danced with considerable effect by Ludmilla Tcherina and Milorad Miskovitch and won the plaudits of the large house.

Yet it is questionable if it outdid in popularity the delightful dancing of Helene Trailine and Jean Bernard Lemoine in the *pas de deux* from Copellia. Mlle. Trailine is already well established as a favourite with Dublin audiences; and M. Lemoine is now as well established, both as soloist and *danseur noble.*

I imagine there will be mixed opinions concerning the ballet *Bonaparte.* Serge Lifar's choreography, obviously influenced by mid - European sources, suffers from an absence of style that follows from the directness of the symbolism.

This added to the effect caused by Ludmilla Tcherina's dancing the part of Napoleon to Beethoven's immortal funeral march, produces an atmosphere of incongruity which is hard to dispel.

Newspaper photo of Jean Babileé and Claire Sombert

As well as her talented soloists, Milorad Miskovitch and herself (Peter Van Dijk broke his leg at the Paris Opera and did not appear), Jean Babileé was the guest *danseur* for the first week, appearing in Massine's *Divertimento*. Of course we had all been waiting to see him in this dramatic solo and he got quite an ovation even before he danced. We were not disappointed. He danced just before and immediately after the interval, the second appearance being a *pas de deux* with Claire Sombert, choreographed by himself, in a rather unique costume-a 'Sloppy Joe' with white bathing trunks and white ankle socks. Hers was a white swim- suit with a fishtail. Many, many curtain calls were taken before *Mephistovalse* with great dancing by Helene Trailine, Jean Bernard Lemoine and Milko Sparenblok to Liszt music and Lifar choreography.

On the last evening, Stanley McCabe made an announcement that Mlle. Charrat was changing into her 'Swan' costume to give us *Le mort du cygne* as a Thank You to Dublin to end the season. Perhaps because I was that bit closer, I had the impression that this was the most convincing 'death' I'd seen. She got tumultuous applause.

By now I had taken to writing little critiques for myself to keep in my programmes – pretentious rubbish – I'd obviously been unconsciously been imitating the newspaper reviews. I'd become far too knowing and critical and this spoilt my overall enjoyment. However, I did appreciate the chance to see a very different style of ballet, about which I'd only read and it all went down in my notebooks!

Dame Ninette de Valois

Irishwoman who became the mother of British ballet

LAST summer, An Post issued a special purple 30p stamp, bearing a composite portrait of Dame Ninette de Valois, to honour this great Irishwoman's achievements. Yet, ironically, the founder of the Royal Ballet, who died on March 8th aged 102, will always be referred to as "the mother of British ballet". However, to the dancers who worked or trained under her, she will always be known as "Madam".

Born Edris Stannus at Baltyboys House in Blessington, Co Wicklow, on June 6th, 1898, she was the second daughter of Lieut Col Stannus, DSO, and Lilith Graydon-Smith, a distinguished glassmaker and collector of Waterford Glass. She chose her daughter's stage name, for dancers then had to have exotic names, usually Russian-sounding. In this case, Huguenot ancestry, with a historic connection to the French royal house, suggested the name.

However, no royal welcome greeted the birth of a second daughter; her father ordering the ground staff not to light the bonfire intended to announce the arrival of the expected son. Hearing this nine years later, Ninette de Valois retorted that she might light her own, though even she could not have foreseen how it would blaze around the world.

It was first sparked when Mrs Leggett-Byrne, who ran a dance studio in Dublin's Adelaide Road, performed at a party. The seven-year-old insisted on performing a jig taught her by their cook, Kate. Soon afterwards the family was unable to afford the upkeep of Baltyboys and Ninette de Valois was sent to live with her grandmother in Walmer, Kent.

Later, recalling a visit to the house, she wrote in her memoirs, Come Dance With Me (1937): "I feel that here, at the foot of these Wicklow Hills, lies the midnight of the first seven years of my life."

In England, she began training in classical ballet at the Lila Field Academy. She watched Pavlova dance The Dying Swan at the Palace Theatre, and noted down the choreography, which she reproduced later on tour.

She got her first West End role in 1914 as principal dancer in the Lyceum pantomime and was re-engaged there each December throughout the first World War, during which her father was killed at the Somme, when commanding the 7th Battalion of the Leinster Regiment.

By also teaching and playing in summer revue and variety, she earned enough to pay for classes with Espinosa and Cecchetti. In 1921, she toured Europe with the Massine-Lopokova company before joining Diaghilev's Les Ballets Russes in 1923 for two years, chronicled in her book, Invitation To The Ballet (1937).

In 1927, W.B. Yeats invited her to run a ballet school at the Abbey, where she also choreographed and performed in his Plays for Dancers. Then Lilian

Baylis, the formidable and eccentric manager of the Old Vic Theatre, employed her as Shakespearian movement coach and choreographer. This led to the founding in 1931 of the Vic-Wells Ballet Company and School, the latter replacing her London Academy of Choreographic Art, which she had founded in 1926.

In 1935, Ninette de Valois dared, very riskily as it seemed, to make a ballerina of the adolescent Margot Fonteyn. She introduced the great classics into the repertory and set about implementing them with a British repertory.

Of her own choreography, she was the toughest of critics, yet she was responsible for making much of that early repertory very British in character. When Frederick Ashton joined her in 1935 she delegated much of the choreography to him, and in the post-war years made only one ballet for her company, the unmemorable Don Quixote. Yet three of her principal pre-war works have lived on: Job (1931)

The Rake's Progress (1935) and Checkmate (1937).

Under her guidance, the Vic-Wells became Sadler's Wells, with a younger sister, the Sadler's Wells Theatre Ballet, and, in 1946, moved to the Royal Opera House, Covent Garden, becoming the Royal Ballet in 1955.

Kind, sensible and outspoken, Ninette de Valois had absolute integrity. A strict disciplinarian, she demanded no more of her dancers than of herself, continuing to dance until 1937, despite pain from an operation in 1935. The latter, however, led to her long and happy marriage to the Irish surgeon who operated on her, the late Dr Arthur Connell.

She retired as director of the Royal Ballet in 1963, loaded with honours, including a CBE (1947), Chevalier of the Legion d'Honneur (1950) and Dame of the Order of the British Empire (1951). In 1961, she became the first woman to receive the Dutch Erasmus Prize and, in 1964, the first, since Marie Curie, to receive the Albert Medal of the Royal Society. In 1980, she received an Irish Community Award and the British Companion of Honour in 1981.

She directed the Royal Ballet School until 1972, remaining on the board of governors, and becoming patron of Irish National Ballet.

Recently ill-health limited her activities, but she was at a special gala performance in Covent Garden in 1997. At curtain fall, the whole company and school assembled on stage as a spotlight found "Madam" and she received a standing ovation.

Ninette de Valois will be mourned throughout the world of dance, however, her legacy lives on wherever she has danced, directed or taught.

Dame Ninette de Valois (Edris Stannus) born 1898; died March 2001

Ninette de Valois . . . standing ovation at Covent Garden in 1997

Irish Times cuttings on Dame Ninette de Valois on her death in 2001

That summer there was a production called *Braziliana* in the Olympia in July 1955 and what a triumph it was! Exuberant, exhilarating, it was a world away from classical dance, full of Latin passion and *joie de vivre*.

But it did not sway me away from my beloved ballet and in September 1955 the famed Sadlers Wells Theatre Ballet came to the Olympia with the Sadlers Wells Orchestra. Ninette de Valois was the Director with Peggy Van Praag. Ashton's *Les Patineurs* music by Meyerbeer was first performed in February 1937 and was revived, with Brenda Bolton, Maurice Bruce, Miro Zoltan and Johaar Mosavaal amongst the cast. It was a cheerful, enjoyable ballet and was followed by *House of Birds* costumed by Georgiadis, which had been premiered earlier in May of this year 1955. It was my first MacMillan Ballet and I was very impressed by his style of choreography, so different from any other I'd seen, very inventive and not as structured as a sequence of classical steps. John Lanchbery orchestrated the score, and the Orchestra was conducted by Kenneth Alwyn. Quite an experience! *Pineapple Poll* again danced by Brenda Bolton followed. We all knew the Gilbert & Sullivan music and had seen the operetta. Now we had a danced version to enjoy, which one couldn't fail to do. Michael Boulton danced Captain Belaye.

Now my autograph book was filled with new signatures: Bridget Badham, Michael Boldin, Johaar Mosaval, Joan Blakeney, Margaret Knoesen, many of whom I hadn't yet got to know, as only some of the names were 'household'.

Carnaval (Fokine/Schumann) with Michael Boulton as Harlequin, Donald MacLeary as Pierrot, was a Commedia del Arte ballet – a frothy sentimental joyful

Review by 'K' of Sadlers Wells Ballet

piece. I'd read about *Blood Wedding* and seen photos in *Dance and Dancers*. This was a very, very dramatic work, ending in inevitable tragedy. Sara Neil was the Bride and Donald Britton was Leonardo. Anyone who saw this work will not quickly forget the dark brooding impression it left. *Danses Concertantes*, premiered in January 1955 was my second MacMillan ballet, and was a sparkly energetic work – all the dancers were in great form! The Orchestra was conducted by John Lanchbery. He also conducted a full length *Coppelia* which I hadn't seen since 1953. Doreen Tempest was Swanhilda, and Miro Zoltan was Franz with Johaar Mosavaal as Dr. Coppelius. The cast members were becoming more familiar and it was easier to pick out new favourites in the large cast. It was a very different production to that of the International Ballet.

In 1931, the Sadlers' Wells had given their first programme at the Old Vic Theatre, after years of difficulties, a triumph for Ninette de Valois – another of 'our own' from Baltinglass! In September 1938 de Valois had brought Sadlers Wells to Dublin, and now they were appearing again at the Olympia. De Valois had studied with Enrico Cechetti and had danced with Diaghilev. She had left to partner Dolin in 1926. As is well known she went to become director of what is now England's Royal Ballet, based at Covent Garden, becoming a Dame in 1951. She died in 2001, having received many other honours in her lifetime. Margot Fonteyn recounts that Dame Ninnette told her that in her own dancing days she took two aspirin, a hot bath and a glass of sherry to relax before a performance!

Still Queueing! Photograph of the author with Irene Kyffin, neé Taylor

'K' considered that de Lorcas *Blood Wedding* 'could not be balletised', but was enthusiastic about *Danses Concertantes*. And the *Irish Independent* music critic enjoyed *Pineapple Poll* (Cranko) and the contrast provided by MacMillan's *House of Birds*. He remarked on the 'syncopated' version of the National Anthem. Those were the days when it was played at every performance, and indeed ended every cinema show. The reverse side of the review noted that M.A. Gannon of County Tyrone had died aged 106, mourned by 31 grandchildren; 24 great grandchildren and 2 great-great grandchildren. Ni beid a leitheid ann aris! Gabriel Fallon writes of the artsy atmosphere. He it was who noted the Sadlers Wells visit in 1938 but makes no further reference to the programme given then. "R.J." was very taken with Doreen Tempest as Coppelia and Seamus Byrne expressed delight in seeing – again – de Valois *The Rakes Progress* and he pays tribute to the interpretation of Elaine Fifield in *Les Sylphides*.

Sadlers Wells paid a return visit in December 1955. Elaine Fifield, Sara Neil and Margaret Hill danced *Les Sylphides* with Miro Zoltan. Ninette de Valois' *The Rakes Progress* with Whistler costumes and Gavin Gordon score was not new to Dublin, but certainly new to me. There were six scenes in this bawdy but ultimately sad ballet, danced enthusiastically by all the company. Another new ballet with a romantic theme, *Saudades* ended the evening. Not my favourite ballet though.

The Olympia was turning out to be THE ballet venue and we got used to queuing at Sycamore Street and nipping over to Bewley's of Georges Street for snacks and hot drinks. Bovril was popular and warming! It was nearer to the 46A terminus, thus one could stay longer at the Stage Door! We also had begun to recognise each other as real ballet supporters and had got to the stage of discussion on the merits of the different companies and dancers.

By now there were a number of fans with whom I went to performances at different times. My friend Irene Taylor, a very knowledgeable balletomane, was someone with whom I went very often, as well as friends Valerie Little, Michelle Costelloe and Clodagh Power and neighbours Noirin Power and Mairin Caffrey. Most of us got the same bus home.

At the start of May 1955 the Desmond Domican Academy of Dance presented an Evening of Ballet at the C.I.E Hall and we had the chance to see Ireland's dancers in a variety of short pieces. Aileen Geelan, Marie Doyle and Bernie Keogh danced in a *pas de trois*, followed by Marie Rice with Junior Corps. Deirdre O'Connor, (listed in my *Collins Ballet Diary* of 1975 as having a birthday on 9 June), and Claire Deen all danced in this production concluding in a Fiesta with Aileen Geelan, Desmond Domican and Senior Corps. Desmond Domican had been a pupil of Marie Rambert. I have no record of reviews myself, but I am certain it got the recognition it deserved. I certainly enjoyed the evening.

And on 3 July 1955 there was a Recital at the Olympia of the Irish National Ballet School, under the direction of Valentina Dudko. Again, it was a series of solos or *pas de deux*. I remember in particular Eistir O Brolochain, Kathe Herkner, Cliodna O'Riordan and Janet Neesham. James Lawlor and Thomas Slevin danced and before the second interval, there was a 'new' *Carnaval*, choreographed by Dudko, taking into consideration the artistic and physical scope of the dancers. Dudko herself danced a Chopin *Mazurka* and, partnered by Thomas Slevin, *Danse Exotique* to close the programme. Given the difficulties encountered by Ballet in Ireland, this was a creditable and ambitious production in a large theatre even at a time when Ballet was on a high of popularity.

The programme advertises the Paradiso Restaurant, of happy memory, which was a fairly sophisticated alternative to hotel restaurants and cinema grillrooms and had three different levels of dining areas, which offered a great and affordable variety of meals. It catered for couples and groups of girls on a night out. It featured many photographs of theatrical personalities who had dined there. The programme also mentions the Harcourt St. Shoe Store, where I got my own ballet shoes (Anello and David or Freed and Gamba) and purchased my double- sided silk/satin ribbons (as preferred by Margot Fonteyn).

1956 was to see the return of Ballets de France and an All-Star Festival of French Ballet. Ludmilla Tcherina gave us her version of the *Dying Swan*, very expressive and sensitive, she gave a very personal interpretation of the death of the swan, but I preferred Charrat's version. Guest star was Boris Trailine.

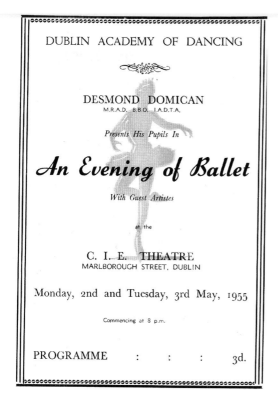

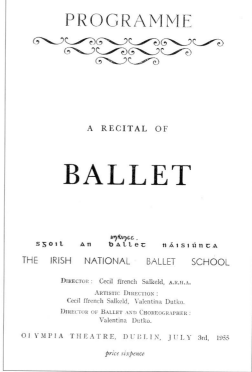

Programme of Irish National School of Ballet recital   Programme of Dublin Academy of Dancing

John Taras' *Design for Six* was new to me and after the interval, Tcherina and Miskovitch danced the Tchaikovsky *Romeo and Juliet* (Lifar) which was very moving. The 'French' version of the *Grand Pas* from the Nutcracker (Casse-Noisette) is one that I have never got used to. It just goes to show that, for some of us, the 'first' version is the original and best. Later, I was to note that the visiting Russians danced this 'second' version, but I have always preferred the dramatic entry with the ballerina with her back to the audience in an extended *developpé*.

Miskovitch danced *L'après midi d'un Faune* which suffered from the smaller Olympia stage. I liked the *Valse de Ravel*.

For the second week there was *First Symphony* (Charrat) followed by now expected *Pas de Quatre* and the *Dying Swan*. Liane Daydé danced in the second part of the week, partnered by Peter Van Dijk. Now readers can see the long list of works new to Dublin and that of visiting guest artists continues to grow.

A rare novelty arrived in the capital in June 1956 – The Royal Danish Ballet came to the Gaiety for one week and presented *Les Sylphides* with Kirsten Simone and Henning Kronstam in the *pas de deux*, the company dancing to the piano of

Danish Ballet at Gaiety

JUDGING by the reception given last night by a large audience at the Gaiety Theatre to the distinguished soloists from the Royal Danish Ballet, the chances of getting seats for the remainder of the week are likely to fall only to the expeditious and the swift. This fact is a measure of the occasion.

The work of the Danish soloists is remarkable for its precision, style and finish. There is, in addition, the delightful small surprises of August Bournonville's choreography. Last night the programme opened with the dances from *Les Sylphides*, in which **Kirsten Simone, Kirsten Ralov, Mette Mollerup** and **Henning Kronstam** made manifest the finer points of the Danish style. There was a poetic rendering of the Nocturne and the Prelude, Mazurka, and Pas de Deux were outstanding.

Fine dancer

The *Fokine* offering was followed by the delightful Pas de Deux from *Flower Festival* in *Genzano*. Here we got our first taste of the Bournonville choreography (to Paulli's music) and, partnering Kirsten Ralov, we took the measure of that very fine dancer Fredbjørn Bjørnason.

Dream Pictures followed the Pas de Deux: a delightful piece of romantic nonsense, replete with quiet humour and danced with evident relish by the entire company. Bjørnason's Harlequin and Inge Sand's Columbine tended to steal the piece, though not quite. The Valse Pas de Deux by Kirsten Ralov and Stanley Williams came unforgettably into the picture as did the Zuav Galop by Mette Mollerup and Henning Kronstam.

But speaking for myself I would have welcomed an encore and yet another encore of the delicate humour projected by Bjørnason and Kirsten Ralov in the Sylphides Valse.

Of one mind

After the interval we had Inge Sand and Stanley Williams in the *Black Swan* pas de deux. Individual balletomane may have other opinions about this interpretation but the Gaiety audience was of one mind on the matter

last night. Then a Pas de Trois (Mollerup, *S i m o n e* and *Oh Fatumi*), f r o m *La Ventana*, another delightful piece of Bournonville choreography and beautifully danced.

Perhaps Sand and Bjørnason were at their best as Swanilda and Frantz in the *Coppelia* extract which followed. The evening finished on a lively note with the entire company clearly diverting themselves as w e l l as the audience in *Pas de Sept* with *Italian Soli*, followed by *Joy of Life*. It goes without saying that there were many, many curtain calls.

A feature of this Danish presentation was the piano playing of Elof Nielsen, who provided the entire musical accompaniment. His offerings of Chopin, Liszt, Sibelius and Grieg during the short intervals between the dances appealed even to those exclusive persons who have grown a little tired, perhaps, of poor Chopin and Liszt. All roads should lead to the Gaiety this week. Most likely they will.

GABRIEL FALLON.

Review of the Danish Ballet company by Gabriel Fallon

IS BRUHN THE GREATEST?

HE BRINGS A NEW MOOD TO BALLET

"OH, but you must see Erik Bruhn, he is the greatest," Inge Sand, of the Royal Danish Ballet said to me two years ago. Bruhn had introduced a new mood to ballet, a sort of majestic mockery suitable to the cynicism of the present times.

This *Epalement* was done with his eyes laughing over his shoulder at the audience, as he unleashed the most intricate movements across the stage.

Now Bruhn, a Dane, is at the Olympia Theatre, Dublin, with the American Ballet Theatre. Last week in Pas de Deux from "Don Quixote" by Leon Minkus. This week he undertakes "Black Swan" and "Giselle."

Precise flip

In a second, after he appeared on the stage one sensed his greatness. There was the precise last-second flip of the hands, as the arms slid into position (like a joint clicking into place) and the calm watchful arrogance in the poise of his splendidly built body.

Then the movements began, graceful and sure at first, till he came out in his first variation and the familiar sensation of exhilaration when one is beholding a great dancer began to revive.

Here was sensational speed, his pirouettes were so fast at one point that the orchestra could not keep up with the dancer. But always Bruhn has supreme control; as he comes to the end of even the

fastest series, his body freezes suddenly into poise and perfect immobility.

Speed combined with such clean precision in the *denouement*, is what marks the great dancer. Bruhn's *entrechats* also had a swift delicacy like the flutter of swan's wings in the moment before it begins to lift from the water.

"Fall River Legend" a piece about a harridan who splits her parents with a hatchet, does not seem to me a ballet at all. Ballet must tell its tale through the movement of the dance alone.

This is the problem the choreographer has to grapple with; how to invent a mechanism, which will create in our minds the illusion that we are watching real life, whereas in fact we are watching life as it is depicted for us through the medium of movement.

Broken illusion

In the same way the painter uses perspective to disguise from us the fact that we are looking at a flat canvas. But in "Fall River Legend" the illusion was constantly broken.

Firstly the piece began by a narrator speaking dialogue. This is a mortal sin in ballet. Then the *corps de ballet* began to mouth the lip movements for songs, without actually singing and near the end there were moments when the music stopped and the dancers just walked round the stage; so that the last vestige of ballet illusion vanished.

ULICK O'CONNOR

Review of Erik Bruhn

Elof Nielson. I never tire of *Sylphides* and relished seeing the Danish ballerinas and corps dancing. Although they had never before been to Dublin, I was familiar with many of the names and faces from the ballet magazines. So, Kirsten and Mette Mollerup were 'known' to me as the curtain rose. The August Bournonville style was apparent in the *pas de deux* from *Flower Festival of Genzano. Dream Pictures* was a light-hearted ballet on the style of 'Harlequinade' and showed off the Danes at their most exuberant. I don't remember being impressed by Inge Sand's Black Swan. I have a ridiculous prejudice against fair-haired black swans! I did not think her style was suited particularly well to this arrogant and provocative dance. But in the *pas de deux* from *Coppélia* which she danced with Fredbjorn Bjornsson, she was delightful. The speedy whipped style of the Danes' footwork was well-suited to *Pas de Sept* with Italian Soli. Bournonville ballets comprised the second half of the programme and it was now becoming easier to appreciate this very distinctive style with the full company dancing. *Joy of Life* closed the programme. This performance was very well received by an enthusiastic Gaiety audience. Indeed 'K' was very impressed by the Royal Danes, as was Gabriel Fallon, but was disappointed with the 'light-weight' programme. On account of the dancers being accompanied by Elof Nielson on piano, it would have been difficult to present a full-length work, but I agreed that the Bournonville style needed to be seen in a longer work. Men and women soloists have an equal chance to show off their technique and their speed and lightness is very characteristic.

Also in 1956 Festival Ballet came, not to the Gaiety but to the Olympia, bringing back *Coppélia* danced by Marilyn Burr or Belinda Wright with either Louis Godfrey or John Gilpin. It was a delight to welcome back old favourites and ballet received a good reception. There were quite a few new names in the lesser roles *Homage to a Princess* dedicated to Princess Grace of Monaco was a ballet by Michael Charnley to Stan Kenton music. *Sylphides, Harlinquinade, Napoli* and *Coppélia* were also mounted.

Enchanting Display
Visiting Ballerina

By MARY MacGORIS
"Irish Independent" Music Critic

MARGOT Fonteyn came, and enchanted Dublin by the elegance and style of her dancing in the full-length "Swan Lake" presented by the Theatre . . .

Theatre
Royal

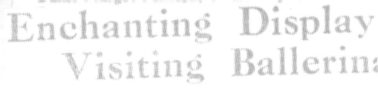

two
New Friends
& Old

The Royal Ballet
American Theatre Ballet
Ballet Bejart

IN "SWAN LAKE"

An uninhibitedly royalist audience gave the recently-warranted former Sadler's Wells Ballet a wildly enthusiastic reception at the Theatre Royal last night, on their first Dublin appearance after 19 years. In the main, the enthusiasm was justified, though I felt a bit irritated when Mr. Robert Irving (Constant Lambert's successor) allowed silly applause to spoil the first announcement of the Swan Motif, the most significant balleto-musical moment in the work, in Act I, which was otherwise memorable only for the Pas-de-Trois of Maryon Lane, Annette Page and Brian Shaw.

"Swan Lake" stands or falls on Act II, and Act II stands or falls on Odette's interpretation. Last night, Margot Fonteyn gave us technique

though perfunctory, carried conviction, bringing great to her Siamese agility and fire artistry in the Grand Pas. In the last Act Pas-de-Deux showed the emotion of Odette for the first time, and her miraculous lightness meticulous wedding of appearance effortless movement to music showed at its best, almost at the applause at the final curtain.

Over all, I must confess my preference for Sergueff's old fashioned carry-over of the original choreography as a better wedding the triple arts that go to the ballet story. I disliked Hurry's rather fussy settings in Act II, when they made the Swans like mostly animated reproductions. I liked better . . .

In May of 1957 the radiance of Britain's Royal Ballet burst upon us when they appeared in Gala mode at the Theatre Royal (Sponsored by Guinness Son & Co.) as part of the International Theatre Festival presented by the Dublin Tostal Council. This was a major coup indeed and an acknowledgment of the extent and discernment of Dublin's appreciation of the ballet. Brendan Smith, Festival Director, we will always be grateful to you for bringing a major world class company with its own orchestra and leading dancers to our capital!

Pre-booking (on Grafton St.) on 1 April saw quite a queue stretching out of sight. Hopefully everyone who wished to go was accommodated as the Theatre Royal held 3,000 people. Almost fainting with relief and exultation on getting the precious tickets into my hand, I wait forty-three days before that exciting first night when we saw Margot Fonteyn, partnered by Michael Somes, dance in *Le Lac des Cygnes* in a version revived by de Valois after Petipa and Ivanov with some additional choreography by Frederick Ashton. I'd been reading up about this famous company, which evolved from Vic Wells roots, and was now resident at the Royal Opera House, Covent Garden. And now we were about to witness them! So many other well-known names also danced that night. Gerd Larsen, Leslie Edwards, Maryon Lane, Anette Page, Antoinette Sibley, Georgina Parkinson, Michael Farley to name but a few with whom I was familiar from books and magazines. Although MILES up in the heights of the Royal far removed from the stage, I was able to get a good view of a big company on a big stage in a major classic, with their prima ballerina, Margot Fonteyn. It is impossible to describe Star Quality. You forget you are watching a famous world- wide name and see only a Swan Queen, and await each act as if one didn't already know the ballet's outcome, experiencing the unfolding of the story through her artistry. Luckily, since I was getting a lift home, I didn't have to rush, and waited with hundreds of others to see her, dressed for a Reception, graciously sign programmes and autograph books, before leaving with Ninette de Valois and Frederick Ashton, both of whom also signed my books. She had arrived with her husband of two years, Roberto de Arias, and she signed my book 'Margot Fonteyn de Arias.'

On the second evening the Company gave *Les Sylphides*. Of course the large stage gave much greater scope to dance more fluently than is possible on a small stage, and could get the impression that the sylphs were wandering in a real glade. There is plenty of space to see the patterns woven by the choreographer and ability to dance to the beauty of the Chopin music unhindered by spatial considerations. Not sure, though, that I don't prefer the more intimate Gaiety stage for this ballet, even if it is restricting.

Two days later, there was a performance of a one-scene ballet by John Cranko (famous for his ingenious 'lifts'- quite acrobatic and modern at that time) *The Shadow*. Philip Chatfield and Meriel Evans danced the leads in this ballet; again with

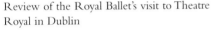

CAST

ACT I

Prince Siegfried	MICHAEL SOMES
The Princess-Mother	GERD LARSEN
Wolfgang, the Prince's Tutor	RAY POWELL
Benno, the Prince's Friend	LESLIE EDWARDS

Pas de Six — MARY DRAGE BRENDA TAYLOR MARGARET MERCIER DESMOND DOYLE RONALD HYND GARY BYRNE

Pas de Trois — MARYON LANE ANNETTE PAGE BRIAN SHAW

A Peasant girl — SHIRLEY GRAHAME

Peasant boys and Huntsmen — DEREK RENCHER DAVID DREW KEITH ROSSON DAVID SHIELDS GRAHAM USHER RICHARD FARLEY KEITH MILLARD DAVID BOSWELL JOHN SALE DOUGLAS STEUART WILLIAM WILSON BASIL THOMPSON BRYAN ASHBRIDGE RONALD PLAISMED CHRISTOPHER NEWTON JOHN STEVENS MAURICE METLISS

Peasant girls — VALERIE TAYLOR CHRISTINE BECKLEY STELLA FARRANCE SALLIE LEWIS ANN HOWARD HYLDA ZINKIN MAVIS OSBORN ANTOINETTE SIBLEY DEBRA WAYNE ANTOINETTE SIBLEY GEORGINA PARKINSON SHIRLEY GRAHAME

Ladies-in-waiting — JENNIFER GAY DOREEN EASTLAKE MARGARET WING JACQUELINE WATCHAM

ACT II

Odette, the Swan Princess	MARGOT FONTEYN
Prince Siegfried	MICHAEL SOMES
Benno	LESLIE EDWARDS
Von Rothbart, a Wicked Magician, in the guise of an owl	ARNOTT MADER

Cygnets — MARYON LANE ANNETTE PAGE JUDITH SINCLAIR DOREEN WELLS

Four Swans — MARY DRAGE BRENDA TAYLOR CATHERINE BOULTON SHIRLEY GRAHAME

Swans — ANTOINETTE SIBLEY MAVIS OSBORN DEIRDRE DIXON STELLA FARRANCE DOROTHEA ZAYMES ANN HOWARD DEBRA WAYNE ANGELA WALTON HYLDA ZINKIN MARGARET WING MARGARET MERCIER JENNIFER GAY GEORGINA PARKINSON SALLIE LEWIS PATRICIA THOROGOOD

Review of the Royal Ballet's visit to Theatre Royal in Dublin

Program for the Royal Ballet's visit to Theatre Royal in Dublin

a cast of high quality soloists with the orchestra being conducted by Robert Irving. *Symphonic Variations* was a much photographed work, choreography by Ashton with costumes by Sophie Fedorovitch to Cesar Franck music. The exquisite Anya Linden, Rosemary Lindsay and Annette Page danced this ballet for soloists with Ronald Hynd, Brian Shaw and Pirimin Trecu. A real 'Dancers' ballet!

The final work was *Ballet Imperial* (Tchaikovsky music and Balanchine choreography). Courtney Kenny was the solo pianist. Brenda Taylor, Judith Sinclair, Gary Bourne and Dereck Rencher were amongst the soloists, all dancing to a uniformly high standard.

A programme note extends thanks to the Alliance & Dublin Consumers Gas Co. Ltd. for providing rehearsal facilities – in D'Olier St., I wonder? On the last night of that stupendous week, I once again saw *Swan Lake*, this time with Nadia Nerina and Alexis Rassine, giving us a chance to see another two first class dancers interpret these roles and the audience an opportunity to 'compare and contrast' – although perhaps this is not a fair comment! The rest of the cast seemed to be the same as on the opening night – Maryon Lane, Annette Page, Judith Sinclair and Doreen Wells danced the cygnets on both evenings.

First lady of Irish ballet

Joan Denise Moriarty.

By Patricia O'Reilly

IN IRELAND today the name Joan Denise Moriarty and the art of professional ballet are synonymous. She is both founder and Artistic Director of the Irish Ballet Company.

It was a strange quirk of fate that made Joan Denise Moriarty set up her ballet school in Cork. The city of Cork was her home, but from the age of six she had trained in London. She returned for a three month stint and with a decision to make — should she continue with her stage career, which would mean living abroad; or return and start ballet in Ireland?

A chance remark from an acquaintance, who likened ballet to "a man chasing a woman across a stage" was the impetus Joan needed to set up her own studio some 31 years ago.

The way was not easy, the beginnings were slow and the work was hard, but slowly the Cork Ballet Group evolved. When their numbers rose to 30, they were renamed the Cork Ballet Company. In 1959 Joan formed a small professional group — The Irish Theatre Ballet, which folded in the '60s because of lack of finance.

Today the parent company, the Irish Ballet Company, which has been in existence for five years, based in Cork, is international, employs a comprehensive staff of 15 and draws its membership from all over the world.

Yesterday Joan Denise Moriarty's original choreographed version of Synge's

"Playboy of the Western World" opened at the Olympia for the 20th Dublin Theatre Festival. She has worked on this production for many years and, though a student of Synge since childhood, has never seen "The Playboy" performed either as a musical or a play.

The music has been composed and is played live by The Chieftains. Paddy Moloney and the group have worked very closely with Joan over the past few months. Indeed, it is one of the few ethnic Irish productions of the Festival.

The ballet is in two acts. The sets have been designed and painted by Patrick Murray, who has also designed the Irish fine hand-woven tweed costumes, which were specially dyed by Dripsey Woollen Mills.

Perhaps a ballet of "The Playboy of the Western World" may seem far removed from the popular classical illusion of ballet. "I do not really use the word 'ballet' much", Joan explains. "I prefer to use the word 'dance', because nowadays a dancer, just like an actor or singer, has to be very versatile and able to perform avant garde electronic scores, rock ballets, jazz ballets and full ballets".

The leading roles of Christy and Pegeen Mike are being danced by Sean Cunningham and Anna Donovan. Sean Cunningham was born in Skibbereen and was a member of the first professional group, the Irish Theatre Ballet. Later he joined the Sadlers Wells Ballet in London, then the Scottish Ballet and later became principal dancer with the Gulbenkian Ballet of Portugal; he subsequently returned to join the Irish Ballet Company and is considered anchor-man of the group.

Anna Donovan is the original member of the Irish Ballet Company and although Irish, lived and went to school in London.

For the first time this year, the Arts Council has granted a scholarship; there were 16 applicants for that one place. To be a dancer in Ireland is no easy task and that is why all but the most dedicated fall by the wayside. Students must train every day and Joan explains the difficulties encountered by pupils from outside Cork, "They have to board out or stay with friends, as I can't take them into the company until they are ready. Occasionally with a promising dancer I have given a year's scholarship, which means that they practise with the company every day—but they must be over 16."

Joan Denise Moriarty feels the only feasible way to train to be a dancer is to go into full-time school. Her plans for setting up a ballet school in Ireland may appear embryonic now, but given even half a chance she will translate them into swift reality.

we wanted to do, to build a library, but we also had to do it. Gael Linn saw there was a need to produce such records, not just for radio but for general consumption. It fulfilled that need, and encouraged the right people in O Riada and Ceoltoirí Chualann. If it never did anything else, it's owed a tremendous debt for what it's done for music".

Ciaran will be leading in the jubilee celebrations this evening with a concert of Sean Nos singing in the New Arts Block in Trinity College. Other events include a story-telling evening on Thursday in the same venue, and on Friday in the Junior Common Room of Trinity, an "Oiche Airreain", featuring light-hearted aspects of a Gaeltacht evening. On Saturday October 9, Peadar O Riada, son of Sean, and his Claisceadal Chuil Aodha will present the songs and music of their own Gaeltacht area in West Cork, also in Trinity.

On Sunday Sean O Riada's second Mass will be sung in St. Saviour's Dominican Church, under the direction of his son, and in the evening there will be a Slogadh concert in the Edmund Burke Theatre in Trinity.

The Silver Jubilee programme will conclude with a concert in the Olympia Theatre on October 15. Heading this will be Miceal O Suilleabhain already being hailed as the new O Riada and one of the most exciting innovators on the traditional scene. He will accompany his wife Noirin Ni Riain, whose album of songs was released some weeks ago by Gael Linn. Also on the programme are Matt Molloy, Paddy Glackin, Triona and Mairead Ni Dhomhnaill, Eamon de Buitlear and Ceoltoirí Laighean. All details of this concert and the jubilee celebrations in general may be had from FONODISC, Telephone 777833.

Newspaper article featuring Joan Denise Moriarty

A complete contrast was *Checkmate* (de Valois/Bliss). It was fitting that another work by de Valois should be given by her company in Dublin. What a fascinating ballet it is, and how ingenious her choreography. The role of the Black Queen was danced by Rosemary Lindsay, with an air of evil menace, and she had a lot of dancing to do! Her make-up (bizarre as seen through the binoculars) was an integral part of her dance/acting and she was quite brilliant. The Red Queen was Anya Linden. The dancing of the Red and Black Pawns was magnificent.

The *Piece d'occasion* (not premiere) was Frederick Ashton's work, *Birthday Offering*, especially choreographed to mark the 25th Anniversary of the Sadlers Wells in 1956. The very striking music by Glazenov and equally striking costumes by Andre Levasseur were perfect vehicles for the fourteen dancers: Margot Fonteyn (in white) was partnered by Michael Soames and Nadia Nerina (in dark green), Rowena Jackson (in red), Elaine Fifield (in black or was it navy?), Anya Linden (in light green), Annette Page, (in blue) and Maryon Lane (in purple) and their partners all made it a real 'Gala Peformance'. The male soloists were Alexander Grant, Brian Shaw, Philip Chatfield, Pirimin Trecu, Bryan Ashbridge, Desmond Doyle, who had not much dancing to do, but partnered ably.

Suddenly, they were gone! I have my programmes and my autograph books containing the signatures of many of the dancers as well as Margot Fonteyn's, Ninette De Valois and Frederick Ashton. I still savour the moment of Margot's first appearance on stage, but only that I have the evidence before me it often seems like a beautiful dream.

I have since read both her autobiography and the recent biography by Meredith Daneman, which describe the ups and downs, the drama and the glamour and the sheer hard work experienced during her career. We were fortunate to see her in Dublin at what many consider was the height of her career. It is amazing at the number of Irish connections there are with world figures in the Dance world. In addition to Ninette de Valois and Anton Dolin, Margot Fonteyn's mother had an Irish mother, and in her autobiography, Dame Margot mentions her Irish characteristics and beauty. Dame Margot Fonteyn died in 1991 and her ashes are interred in the Jardin de la Paz, on the outskirts of Panama City.

By way of complete contrast, *Les Ballets Theatre De Paris De Maurice Béjart* appeared in the Olympia in November 1957. *Chapeaux* featured thirteen dancers including Béjart and was followed by a *pas de deux* danced by Tessa Beaumont and Adolpho Andrade to Grieg music. Then we witnessed the rather frightening 'psychological' ballet *Sonate a trois* based on Jean Paul Sartre's *Huis Clos*. This was danced by Béjart, Michelle Seigneuret and Tania Bari and was a riveting, if depressing depiction of frustration and hell on earth! Another electrifying work *High Voltage* was an amazing production with a violent theme, all danced with great technicality. *Theatre du realité!* This was a two-week programme, which included a world premiere of *'Etudes Techniques'* but I was unable to see this.

Programme advertisements featured Tayto crisps, Mosney Holiday camp and a fascinating invitation to purchase, in Helys of Dame Street, the Empire Aristocrat typewriter, weighing 8 ¾ lbs., standing no higher than a matchbox! Churchmans cigarettes were 3/9d for twenty!!

So in the five years from 1952 the amazing number of performances by the companies recorded shows the great interest in and hunger for, ballet in Dublin during that decade.

No doubt the great pioneering work done by Joan Denise Moriarty in Cork, where she had set up her school and amateur company in 1947 and then Ireland's first professional company in 1959, had whetted the appetite of an Irish audience for ballet, this form of dance, so difficult, yet made to appear so effortless. It was in complete contrast to our Irish dance where very often, but not always, concentration is restricted to lower body movement. This could not be in greater contrast to the fluidity and grace of ballet. Joan Denise Moriarty had brought her company to many venues in Ireland and often in the face of great difficulties both administrative and stage surface-wise. Many teachers had qualified and set up schools in major centres. Naturally, due to the population, most of these schools were in Dublin. Perhaps many of them were also influenced either by attending of hearing of the visit of Pavlova to the Theatre Royal (1930). This fascinating fact was brought to the publics' attention in a review of the Kirov Ballets visit, by Blainid O'Brolochain, - Pavlova having been a member of the Maryinsky Company (now Kirov). Similarly, there was a reference to a pre-war visit by Sadlers Wells in 1938.

However, it seems to me that the 1950s represents the Golden Age of Ballet in Dublin, despite the arrival of the Big Russian Names in the Sixties, Seventies and subsequently. The sheer variety of companies who came to delight and to educate us in their differing styles of dance and of ballets mounted, and their capacity to adapt to Dublin's smaller stages had never ceased to amaze me.

For instance, in June 1958 we had Western Theatre Ballet, whose Patron was Moira Shearer, that beautiful auburn haired Vic Wells ballerina who became famous for her role in the film *The Red Shoes*, at the Gaiety for a week. This was prior to a Sadlers Wells and Continental Tour. They presented *Peter and the Wolf, Girl in a Mask* (choreography by Wolfgang Brunner) and Peter Darrel's *The Enchanted Rose Garden, Pulcinella, Impromptu, The Prisoners, Celeste and Celestinha, Impasse, Tableaux Vivants* and the *pas de deux* from Act 1 of *Giselle* dances by Brenda Last and Ronald Emblen. What variety! Sadly Moira Shearer died in February 2006.

Mary McGoris reviews this season favourably, and mentions *Impromptu* in particular, which I remember being an exuberant romp, which the dancers all enjoyed. Their co-artistic director, Elizabeth West, was enthusiastic both about her own small dedicated company (Peter Darrell is the other director) and also about the possibilities of having an Irish Professional Company. A review by 'K' later in the year refers to a second visit, for which I have no record or memory. Perhaps I was away.

But in July 1958 the American Theatre Ballet paid us a visit under the direction of Lucia Chase and Oliver Smith. Big Names such as Nora Kaye, John Kriza, Erich Bruhn, Lupe Serrano (who later danced with Nurevey), Violette Verdi, Scott Douglas and Royes Fernandez showed the 'American' style, in, amongst other ballets: *Les Patineurs* (Ashton), *Offenbach in the Underworld* (Anthony Tudor) and *Rodeo* (de Mille). Lupe Serrano and Erick Bruhn danced an electrifying *Don Quixote*. 'Is Bruhn the Greatest'? asks Ulick O'Connor, in an article extolling the 'presence, physique and technique' of the superb Danish dancer – another of the Big Names to come to Dublin.

Interplay (Robbins/Morton Gould) was a short four-movement ballet with a short solo for Scott Douglas. Earlier performances, which I did not see, included *Billy the Kid, The Combat, Winter's Eve* and *Fancy Free. Theme*

She hopes to set up professional ballet in Dublin

By ANN B. MURPHY

FOR a number of years Dublin's ballet enthusiasts have deplored the fact that the city has no professional ballet company of its own, although the Dublin ballet schools are filled with pupils. A move has been made to change this with the energy and enthusiasm of a 28 - year - old English girl, Elizabeth West, one of the two Artistic Directors of the newly formed Western Theatre Ballet Company which is due to open a season at the Gaiety, Dublin, next week.

Because a ballet company, run along similar lines as the Western Theatre Ballet company would seem to be the most feasible thing for Dublin at the moment, Irish ballet lovers, headed by Commandant J. C. McGough, have made arrangements for Miss West to lecture in the Gaiety Theatre next Wednesday at 4 p.m.

In addition four Dublin ballet pupils will be allowed to rehearse with the company during their visit to the city.

Dublin ballet-dancing teachers will also be brought together with the chairmanship of Mr. T. A. Doyle of the Dublin Grand Opera Society with the idea of launching some sort of ballet company here and Miss West has agreed to help in any way she can.

Dancers' faith

"It's only by the dancers' faith and our not losing courage that the Company has survived its first year of existence" said Miss West.

"Often the six boys and six girls who comprise the Company have had to take jobs as waiters and washers-up to earn enough to eat and keep the company together when there were no stage bookings " went on Miss West.

"They did not want to see the company break up and took these jobs temporarily, even though they were offered individual jobs with other ballet companies."

Bristol Old Vic

Miss West, who has been devoted to the theatre all her life, has had most of her experience with the Bristol Old Vic, but has always been interested in the production of ballet.

Five years ago with some students from the Old Vic and some from Bristol ballet schools she formed an "amateur" ballet company on a professional status.

The excellence of the three-yearly productions in Bristol so impressed the Arts Council that shen was encouraged to form a real professional company with trained dancers. Joining forces with Peter Darrell, a dancer well known to Dublin audiences, the Western Theatre Ballet.

It is now just one year old and by all accounts it seems well on the road to becoming a permanent company despite the lack of finance which continually raises a problem.

"We have a grant of £500 from the Arts Council", says Miss West, "but it costs £600 alone to pay for just the six girls dancing shoes during one year."

Turning point

"Our Dublin reception could be the turning point in our career," she said. "The fact that we stayed together at all was because of the surprisingly good reception which we got in London when we were only three weeks old."

Since their London performance the ballet company has had odd jobs on TV, in films and during the winter they played in pantomimes and opera.

"It is in this way that I think an Irish ballet company could be arranged," she says. "All that is needed is enthusiasm and the will to keep on no matter what that obstacles. Taking odd bookings during opera seasons, in musical shows, on TV, while getting in some practice together; this is the basis on which we are working.

"The ballets which they perform ? . . . They are mostly all modern and original ballets," said Miss West, who is herself one of the choreographers.

Elizabeth West

Newspaper article featuring Joan Denise Moriarty

and Variations – a Balanchine ballet to Tchaikovsky score was the last night offering of American Theatre Ballet with Violette Verdy and the exciting Royes Fernandez and company. It was a good curtain raiser, followed by *Fall River Legend* with Nora Kaye as the Accused, and Lucia Chase as the Step Mother. History indeed! John Kriza was The Pastor. Erich Bruhn and Lupe Serrano (who had danced with Nureyev) danced an electrifying Don Quixote. They also danced *Les Patineurs* (Ashton), *Rodeo* (de Mille) and *Offenbach in the Underworld* (Tudor) and the Black Swan with Bruhn and Serrano. Once again they presented a wonderful variety, which must be a means of keeping the dancers fresh and challenged.

Ballet programmes for the Olympia changed to a bright red and gold cover, featuring the famous IMP of 'Illsley-McCabe Productions'.

But back to March 1958. Festival Ballet, 'at Home' at the Gaiety! Belinda Wright, so beloved of Dublin ballet-goers was *enceinte*, so her dancing partnership with John Gilpin was just a memory during this season. My programme for Thursday 27 February mentions that Deirdre O'Conaire would be dancing on 28th, but I did not see this performance. *Concerti* (Lichine/Vivaldi) was the first ballet, beautifully danced by all the company, including Ronald Emblen, who had danced with Western Theatre Ballet, all those names and faces now familiar over so many visits. Even a new face in the corps attracted attention!

By this time my little autograph book was filled with the names of these well-loved dancers in addition to the 'Greats' and I treasure them for the continual pleasure they gave. Dublin audiences were becoming more 'educated' but still very appreciative, and the dancers always seemed to recognise this and rose to the occasion whether it was in the Gaiety or the Olympia.

Witch Boy, a vehicle for John Gilpin was danced with great drama and aplomb, the first time I'd seen him dance in such a role. I have already mentioned that I had quite early on taken to writing my own critiques (not always agreeing with Ulick O'Connor, Gabriel Fallen, Mary McGoris or Carolyn Swift but they were MY impressions). My 'records' show that I thought *Witch Boy* was one of the really dramatic ballets danced by Festival Ballet – everything fitting together smoothly, and for me the most successful modern ballet I'd seen to date, with the beautiful Anita Landa portraying Barbara Allen, and Anton Dolin dancing The Preacher in the story of the legend. It was an evening to remember. The drama of the ending with it's shock tactic made for great theatre and I end my 'review' by saying how much I'd like to see it again.

Hard to go wrong with *Graduation Ball*, and good all-round dancing with a cast that included Pamela Hart, Peter White, Jean-Pierre Alban and Andre Prokovsky. Both of the above ballets received Dublin premieres.

The second week's offerings were *Swan Lake* Act 2 with Dolin and Krassovska– a part which suits her 'real' ballerina look and, of course it is always a pleasure to see a true *danseur noble* in action. *The Nutcracker Suite* (Act 2) had John Gilpin and Jeannette Minty in the principal roles. The beautiful Grand *pas de deux* with the familiar entrance showing the ballerina with her back to the audience, never fails to enchant me and I cannot find the same pleasure in the versions presented nowadays. I can easily recapture the absolute magic of that first time I saw this and on this occasion it was just a well danced. Gilpin is a very exciting dancer in technical ease, theatricality and the obvious delight with which he dances and partners.

In addition he danced the Black Swan *pas de deux* with Krassovska, who is brilliant in this part, *fouettés* being no problem to her, nor any other technical difficulties. The male solo is electrifying and of course, Gilpin didn't fail to deliver. It was one of those special performances. I record how well Festival Ballet is always received and note that they were en route to Belfast, Liverpool and Glasgow before embarking on a continental tour. So hard working, like all dancers.

On 6 March, still queuing for the Gods, we were back to see *Giselle* with Krassovska (she was originally from Russia) dancing Giselle with Dolin. Although a Senior by now, his partnering abilities and drama enhance Giselle, one of his favourites, I like to think. Perhaps this is why the Peasant *pas de deux* was excluded, I don't know. These classics suit Krassovska as her acting as well as her dancing is convincing. I remember the corps being particularly light and SILENT – a must for the shade of a bereaved fiancée. André Prokovsky partnered Marlyn Burr in the Black Swan, a performance acclaimed by the *Independent* critic, but not agreed with by me on this occasion. *Symphony for Fun* remains one of my favourite ballets and the company gave it their all in the finale. Bravo, Landa, Gilpin and Minty.

Ballet Rambert paid us a welcome return visit in October November 1958, with the wonderful Beryl Goldwyn and John Chesworth and Lucette Aldous. Tudor's *Lilac Garden* - a modern classic – was given before the interval and *Death and the Maiden* (Andree Howard) followed. It was my first time seeing it, with June Sandbrook and John Chesworth. Another Tudor Ballet, *Judgement of Paris* preceded *Two Brothers* (choreographer Norman Morrice, who danced The Brother). What a coup for a choreographer to dance in his own ballet. All credit to the Polish Mme. Marie Rambert, who also caused intense excitement when she gave classes and explained the physical and spiritual requirements for a dancer. Yet another Tudor *Gala Performance* with Prokofiev music depicts the three ballerinas from the Russian, Italian and French schools vying with each other – a burlesque, so enjoyable, and excellently danced by Goldwyn, Elsa Recagno and Lucette Aldous. A sure fire curtain caller!

I think it was on this occasion that Mme. Rambert took a class and conducted auditions. I'm told that she had strict criteria for a dancer – which was that he/she must be a dancer from head to toe! This programme advertises the infamous Shanahan Stamps Investment Plan and heralds the forthcoming R& R production of *Bitter Sweet*. 1959 was a busy year for me personally, the ballet highlight of which was a performance by the Royal Ballet at Covent Garden in April (*The Lady and the Fool* with Beriosova (who had not come to Dublin) Ronald Hynd, Ray Powell and Leslie Edwards. *Harlequin* in April with David Blair and Doreen Wells as Columbine, my first *Petrushka*, with Brian Shaw and Nadia Nerina as the Ballerina. This was a really exciting and dramatic ballet.

If any companies came to Dublin in the first half of the year, I missed them. But in September the Theatre Festival brought 'our' Festival Ballet back to Dublin to the Theatre Royal with the London Philharmonic Orchestra, conductor, Geoffrey Corbett /Aubrey Bowman. A world premiere of a Ballet in one scene by Anton Dolin to a scenario by Miceal MacLiammoir with music by Debussy brought life to the *Legend of Wandering Aengus*, in a new way for me. Yvette Chauviré danced in Act 2 of *Swan Lake*, partnered by Vladimir Skouratoff, and this was yet another opportunity to see a major international ballerina dance in a classical role. She was not helped by her partner, according to Mary McGoris, who was probably seated nearer to the stage than I was. Once again, the corps, being allowed the freedom of a large stage, excelled themselves.

London Morning by Noel Coward, Choreography by Jack Carter was a special project of Anton Dolin's and he was very pleased to bring it to Dublin. He himself played the Man in the bath chair. However it got a poor review from Mary McGoris. I enjoyed it as a new work and enjoyed the vignette of Dolin's performance but felt no particular desire to see it again.

Concerti, still in the repertoire bears repeated viewing however, especially on the large stage, whereas Dolin's interpretation of *Bolero* was more suited to the smaller Gaiety one. (Joan Denise Moriarty had also danced a solo to the Ravel music).

Another well-known ballerina, not yet seen in Dublin, Carla Fracci, danced in Harliniquade with John Gilpin –and *Symphony for Fun* went down very well with

---

BALLET RAMBERT EXCEL IN "GISELLE"

"Giselle," the only full-length ballet presented by the Ballet Rambert in their current season at the Gaiety Theatre is unquestionably their finest production, and is one of the most touching productions of this ballet which Dublin has seen.

Beryl Goldwyn, a dancer in the romantic tradition, gave an exquisite performance as Giselle, full of joyous innocence in Act One, and of radiant tenderness in Act Two.

She dances with grace and lightness and a beautifully flowing line; her lovely porte-de-bras and the graceful carriage of her head made her, in Act Two, seem truly the spirit she portrayed.

The work of the *corps-de-ballet* also was excellent, precise and smooth, and Margaret Hill, as the Queen of the Wilis, brought ease and style and an admirable cold inhumanity to a part which often seems merely athletic.

DUCAL BEARING

As Albrecht, Alexander Bennett had a ducal bearing, and danced finely as well as partnering in his usual admirable fashion. Norman Dixon is the best Hilarion I have ever seen, gaining sympathy for the wretched gamekeeper, whose understandable jealousy precipitates the tragedy which Albrecht's selfishness has caused.

One wonders why so many lovers of ballet music appear to despise this ballet's expressive and touchingly simple score; the orchestral performance, though still shaky as to intonation, was an improvement on previous efforts.

"Love Knots," a Directoire trifle with an attractive setting by Ronald Ferns, had a gay performance by Patricia Ashworth, and an appealing one by Noreen Sopwith, who also distinguished herself with Ronald Yerrell in the *pas-de-deux* from "The Nutcracker."

"Death and the Maiden," finely danced by Margaret Hill and John Chesworth to music from Schubert's D Minor Quartet, owes something to Kurt Joos' "Green Table," and nothing at all to the sad-coloured costumes designed by the choreographer, Andree Howard.

M. MacG.

Dublin Theatre Festival

OFF TO GALA START WITH BALLET

IN spite of the preliminary "commercial," very suavely spoken by Lord Killanin, Festival Ballet sent the Dublin Theatre Festival off to a gala start at the Theatre Royal. Last night's was a most generous programme with such an embarrassment of balletic riches that it is hard to know where to begin, but Markova's Dying Swan will remain in my mind for a long time.

It is probably unfair to make comparisons with Pavlova's interpretation which I have seen only on indifferent film, but Markova's tragic romantic intensity, her elegiac realisation of the rôle, and the lyric beauty of her arms, elevated Saint-Saen's trite music and the melodramatic choreography into something touching and memorable.

Coward's first ballet, "London Morning," has been treated rather patronisingly by some socially-conscious London critics. Approached in an non-L.S.E. way it offers exuberent and immensely satisfying entertainment, nearly as good as an English "Gaieté Parisienne" or a neo-Elizabethan "Pineapple Poll." Coward's score, indeed, in its mood, is heavily in debt to Sullivan, but who cares—it is gay and happy—qualities that are happily reflected in Carter's choreography, William Constable's brilliant set, and N o r m a n McDowell's divinely ridiculous costumes. Louis Godfery and Jeanette Minty share the comic-romantic leads; Dolin has his own comedy score as an ald gent in a bathchair tormented by St. Trinian's girls; Peter White is the essence of all London "Bobbies," and there is a superb bit of business with House Guards, superbly officered by Vassilie Trunoff to fine full-throated brass from the London Philharmonic Orchestra, who were more confident in this than in some other items last night. The whole thing is glorious fun and a fine vehicle for a company which enjoys it, which is as much as it is meant to.

Yvette Chauviré, who opened last night's programme with Act II of "Swan Lake," was damned with faint raises—if I may coin the phrase. In the big duets her partner seemed very uncertain; his lifts were far from sure, and his lack of security seemed to transmit to the Odette, a very fine dancer normally, so that her solos were less than whole-hearted, though one occasionally glimpsed the fine Chauviré line, and the back like a tautly-drawn bow-string. In this "Swan Lake," the Swan leaders of Deirdre O'Conaire and Mary Duchesne, and the well-drilled Corps stole most of the thunder.

For pure dancing, the high-spots of the night, after Markova, were the two *Pas-de-deux* (Drigo and Minkus), danced respectively by Carla Fracci and John Gilpin and Toni Lander and André Prokovsky. Gilpin, incredibly, improves with every appearance here. Fracci is beautiful, a comedienne, and a fine technician as well. Toni Lander had one beautiful solo. Her partner, Prokovsky, has a technique only overshadowed by Gilpin's, with enormously powerful lifts. Both these *divertissments* were clean, crisp, confident dancing at its best, and both got well-deserved ovations.

"Symphony for Fun," last night's savoury, was a delight, as always, with Minty, Anita Landa, Gilpin, and Keith Beckett (a dancer we should see more of this season) leading with their usual *iole de vivre* in which Geoffrey Corbert and the L.P.O. whole-heartedly shared.

One grouse. However enthusiastic they may be, ballet audiences would serve the art, the artists, and fellow members of the audience better if they would refrain from disruptive applause on individual entrances and before the finish of solos.   K.

Dublin Festival Review

the audience, as always. Lander and Prokovsky danced in *Don Quixote*. And, as a very special offering, Alicia Markova danced the Dying Swan. Large stage or no, she was the very essence of a creature losing its grip on life and 'expired' before our very eyes.

'K' on the whole, was very positive about all the evening's offerings, mentioning Toni Lander in her *pas de deux* and praising Markova and legitimately grousing about the spontaneous applause that Dublin audiences are apt to give very to at inopportune moments. Knowing from Dolin's autobiography just how difficult Markova could be, it was a triumph to have cajoled her to Dublin for yet another performance. And Chauvirè too! A newspaper photo pictures Chauvire (France), Burr (Australia) Markova (Britain), Fracci (Italy) and Lander (Denmark). Lord Killanin, as Chair of the Theatre Festival, must be credited with bringing these artists

ARTISTS IN THEATRE FESTIVAL

Visiting artists for the Dublin International Theatre Festival at yesterday's press conference in the Shelbourne Hotel (left to right): Yvette Chauviré (France), Marilyn Burr (Australia), Alicia Markova (Britain)), Carla Fracci (Italy) and Toni Lander (Denmark).

to the capital. What a fantastic decade of ballet in Dublin. The current popularity of the dance in Dublin, was estimated by the number of people who were disappointed at not getting tickets. Those in the know booked immediately.

The era of The Gods in the Gaiety were to end with the refurbishment of the theatre, and is looked back at with great nostalgia. Was there ever such an atmosphere as when the enchanted audience shouted the bravos, stamped against the wooden seats as they begged for encores, which were so often so generously given? The rush down to the favourite seat, the smell of the make up and the resin, even from behind the Safety Curtain, and the sounds of the orchestra tuning up. What happy memories to bring into the 1960s!

three

1960s

Irish Theatre Ballet
Touring Royals
Miskovitch etc.

In May of 1960, the touring section of the Royal Ballet appeared in the Gaiety and presented Nadia Nerina and David Blair in the *Sleeping Beauty*. Never my favourite amongst the classics, despite the wonderful score, it was the original performance of Claudie Algeranova that contained the most magic for me, although of course the Royal Ballets soloists were excellent. Pirimin Trecu was excellent despite a fall in his solo. 'K' was not very impressed with the whole performance either. But Gabriel Fallen gave it good marks! They also presented *Coppélia, Les Sylphides, Blood Wedding* and *Pineapple Poll*. Anne Heaton was principal guest artist. The principals of this touring section of the company were: Nadia Nerina, Anya Linden, Susan Alexander, Antoinette Sibley, Donald Britton, David Blair and Pirimin Trecu – all dancers of the finest quality.

The Wimpy (Bar) Snackery, 10 Burgh Quay, featured, alongside Thwaites 'original' soda water in its flagon – popular for over 180 years, we noted, as we read through the programme. *Les Sylphides*, a production by S. Grigoriev and Luba Tchernikova was a variant on by previous experiences. Susan Alexander and Alexander Bennett danced the *pas de deux*.

Ballet Rambert at the Gaiety

IT is difficult to believe that it is but three years short of half a century since the distinguished lady whose talented young company warmed up before a cold house at the Gaiety Theatre last night beat time for Nijinsky's rhythmically moving groups in "Le Sacre du Printemps."

What a whirl of great dancers and choreographers have passed through her hands since then, many of them blooming in the golden thirties of the Mercury Theatre.

Last night's Ballet Rambert programme opened with an intriguing one act ballet "Two Brothers" an economically told short story with some very fine choreography by Norman Morrice, whose mime and movement as the more operative brother was outstanding.

He was excellently supported by Gillian Martlew, John Chesworth and a promising corp de ballet; and most suitably served by Ralph Koltai's evocative décor and costumes.

Wears well

The 90-year-old "Coppelia" may be the least important of the classics, but it wears well for all that. No doubt, its attraction lies in the moments of brilliant dance it enshrines, as well as the appeal of the romantic music of Delibes.

It is next to no time since we saw it on the Gaiety stage, and so it is a particular tribute to the Ballet Rambert that we were anything but bored last night.

In the first place, I found the Doboujinsky décor and costumes by far the most satisfying I have yet seen. Act II was particularly effective, and a considerable advance on earlier settings.

Warmed up

There was a little uncertainty in the dancing in the opening Act; generally, it lacked precision. But then the dancers warmed up and brought the house to their feet long before the final appreciative curtain.

Lucette Aldous was an excellent Swanhilda. She had vivacity and speed without that flashing perkiness which tends to spoil so many interpretations of this role. Kenneth Bannerman's Franz proved, not only that he is a dancer of much promise, but that he is an excellent partner as well — a rather important distinction.

Pas-de-deux

This was particularly evident in the third act pas-de-deux in which Miss Aldous scored heavily. Norman Morrice's Dr. Coppelia was a delightful piece of miming, mainly because Mr. Morrice, unlike so many other performers in this part, elected to give us rather more character than caricature.

June Sandbrook's Dawn and Gillian Martlew's Prayer were, with the pas-de-deux, the most outstanding items in the third Act.

By the time the final curtain fell, the audience was frantically enthusiastic. Probably their enjoyment—did they know it ?—came as much from the marked potential of these young dancers of Marie Rambert's training, as from their actual achievement last night.

But this — let there be no mistake about it—was considerable. I look forward to Thursday's "La Sylphide" with no little excitement.

GABRIEL FALLON

Gabriel Fallon Review of Marie Rambert

Blood Wedding had been lauded in advance. Very brooding and despairing, though dramatically danced by Donald Britton and Anne Heaton and Audrey Farris. Gabrial Fallon was greatly taken with *Sylphides*. He was less enthusiastic about *Blood Wedding*, though he applauded the soloists, but he thoroughly enjoyed *Pineapple Poll*, the final ballet, and who could not? Britton as Captain Belaye, Audrey Farris as Poll and Johaar Mosaval as Jasper were in fine form and the whole company rose to the rousing Sullivan (arranged by MacKerras) music and the Cranko choreography.

October 1960 and Ballet Rambert was back! With their orchestra under David Ellenberg, Lucette Aldous heads the company. Gabriel Fallon reminds us that Mme. Rambert was almost half a century away from her appearances in the Nijinsky Ballet *Le Sacre du Printemps*.

Two Brothers, so powerful and well received two years ago with Morrice again dancing his own work opened the season and was followed by *Coppélia* in which he played Dr Coppelius. Coppélia was Gayrie Mac Sween, a dancer not familiar to me and Kenneth Bannerman was Franz. I recorded my dislike for the costumes and wasn't too happy with the orchestra on the night. However, Lucette Aldous as Swanhilda was outstanding (she alternated the role with Shirley Dixon) and her performance lifted the whole night. *Czernyana* (Choreography Frank Staff) was given, I can't recall much of this ballet except the *Nuages* of Jennifer Kelly and John Chesworth. I should remember Elsa Recagno, who had danced in *Gala Performance*, but perhaps I was looking too much ahead to *La Sylphide* – a Bournonville ballet set in Scotland, with music by Loven Skjold. It was a romantic and dramatic story with a doomed bride, fallen wings and an unhappy ending. The Bournonville style, seen in short works given by the Danish ballet, was now seen in a full work. Lucette Aldous, of the exceptional lightness, hardly need the wires to float heaven-ward, or up a chimney! Bannerman was a bit disappointing, though Shirley Dixon and John Chesworth were good as secondary characters. Mme. Rambert gave a brief speech of thanks to end the season.

1961 – I did not go to any ballet performance in a theatre this year, but it was the year of that famous Recital in the Mansion House, when many teachers combined to mount what was known as *The Demonstration*. This gave great exposure to the teachers and pupils. It was a monumental production, which received great acclaim.

Ballet Miskovitch de Paris came to the Olympia in 1962. Curiously, the programme gave neither date nor year – I have written 12.5.62 on the inside. He had danced here with Festival ballet, and had partnered Markova, and now with his own company he presented *Le Rideau Rouge*, with Janine Monin, Nicole Nogaret, Ramon Sole, Michael Nunes, Claudie Jacquelin, Larry Haider - all new names to me. The choreographer was John Taras, music by Blareau and Andre Levasseur designed the costumes. So it was a very effective and pleasing ballet, plotless in a fantastical and romantic vein. Miskovitch danced the Grand Pas from Casse-Noisette with Zenia Palley (nee McMahon, according to 'K'). The pianists Jacqueline Emery and Kresimir Sipsuh, accompanied on the piano, all the dancers. *Senor le Manara* (Tchaikovsky, Carter choreography) was one of those introspective and tortured themes giving dramatic scope to the dancers. *Cherche Partenaire* (Bett, Reich) was a 'competition' ballet - always interesting, as various styles are portrayed. *Suite Lyrique* (Vassili Sulich) for six dancers to Grieg music was in classical style, which I always enjoy. Janine Monin, a neat technical dancer danced Don Quichotte with fire and passion with Michael Nunes who was a bit hesitant. *Prometheus* was a Béjart ballet, which was always worth seeing and this one, dealing with a mythical theme full of symbolism and drama need good dancing to do it justice and Miskovitch himself danced Prometheus. *Suite en Blanc* (Lifar/Lalo) came after *Prelude a l'après-midi d'un Faune* danced by Miskovitch in 'civvies'. A novel costume, that made us all sit up! An interesting *pas de deux* for Palley and Haider, followed, they made a good team.

A notice at the conclusion of 'K's review informed us that Maureen Potter was 'pottterin' around for the third time at the Theatre Royal and *The Ninth Day* was retained at the Gate, while the *The Chalk Garden* was playing at Dun Laoghaire's Gas Company Theatre, and *Cat on a Hot Tin Roof* was at the Eblana – the latter venues only happy memories.

The second programme gave us *Guillaume Tell* (Rossini) with Miskovitch choreography. This was a *pas de trois* and a *pas de six* for the company. The *pas de deux* from Swan Lake (no act specified: it was Act two) was given before the interval, and *L'Echelle* (The Ladder) afterwards. This was another dramatic murder-theme ballet in which the three characters dance their own version of events. Intriguingly different! *Romeo and Juliette* (Tchaikovsky) ended the evening, the pianos not quite the best accompaniment to this tragic-romantic ballet.

On April 1 1962 Irish Theatre Ballet (Cork) gave a season at the Gate Theatre which has a rather small stage –not too great a disadvantage for a small company presenting works not requiring any great demands en l'air (apart from the *Don Quixote*). ~~*Suite for no male dancers*~~ with choreography by Denis Carey to Bartok music in which Julia Cotter, Kay McLoughlin and Irene Dayer danced a vaguely folksy set of dance/exercises. The company was happier dancing *West Cork Ballad* accompanied by Reachtaire an Riadaigh with a strong traditional flavour that suited the company. Domy Reiter was The Strolling Fiddler with Julia Cotter as the girl unable to stop dancing to his Tunes. The Grand Pas from *Don Quixote* is ambitious. Joahne O'Hara, to my mind, was the star of the company and carried off this difficult dancing with bravaura and assurance. Also featured were, *Bitter Aloes*, a ballet of tragic emotions choreography Geoffrey Davidson), *Valse Triste* to that haunting Sibelius music again featuring Joahne

O'Hara with Death being danced by Geoffrey Davidson to Joan Denise Moriarty's choreography.

After the interval, during which the audience was buzzing with reaction to a professional Irish company's achievements, the company presented *Moods*, (choreography Reiter), a jazzy, highly spirited ballet which both dancers and audience enjoyed. Nothing beyond the scope of the company was attempted and all the dancers seemed to relax and enjoy. Many Irish dancers, though well endowed compared with dancers from the continent and Britain, are extremely light on their feet and, while not attempting major ballon land gracefully and SILENTLY.

The second programme gave *Figure of Fun*, *Cry Havoc* and *Il Cassone* in addition to those already presented, but I didn't see this performance. The Saturday matinee presented *Coppélia* Act Two and was danced with great aplomb. However, the short tutus do not suit all our girls, and a slightly longer length style might have been more effective. Geoffrey Davidson was a good Dr. Coppelius.

Sugrai Sraide again showed the Company in a Joan Denise Moriarty ballet and was one with which they were happy to show off her choreography. Thomas Kelly and E. J. Moeran composed the score and there was plenty of spirited ensemble dancing on the steps of the old Cork Opera House.

Irene Dayer and Domy Reiter danced the *pas de deux* from *Giselle* a pleasing dance but difficult to take out of context, unlike other major grand pas. This season was a major triumph for Joan Denise Moriarty and her dancers and deserves to be acknowledged as such, presenting as it did as varied and ambitious a programme as any other company visiting the capital. 'K' gave a good review, specially the second programme.

In November 1962 Festival Ballet came for a two- week season at the Olympia. Guest artists were Irina Borowska and Georges Goviloff. John Gilpin is listed as Artistic Director and the Festival Ballet Orchestra was directed and conducted by Aubrey Bowman. Jean-Pierre Alban and Vassili Trunoff were there, joined by some new faces – and feet!

Les Sylphides was recently reproduced by Alicia Markova and given under its original title of *Chopiniana*. Diaghilev changed it to *Les Sylphides* in 1909 when Pavlova, Karsavina, Baldina and Nijinsky danced it. What an inspiration! 'K' tells us that the present company's opening night was bedevilled by a blizzard, which hampered their journey through England and that, on arrival the Company's costumes, shoes and musical instruments were still in Newcastle! Perhaps it was the relief of their eventual arrival and that 'the show must go on' mentality, but it was a calm and musical *Sylphides* that we saw with Borowska, Mathé, Minty and Barry McGrath. Estelle Nova danced the Mazurka on Tuesday as did Desmond Kelly. A few Irish names, including Anna Delaney were appearing now and again in the company.

The Gallery in the Olympia was still unreserved at 3/- and this was where we were installed during the season. *The Black Swan* Grand *Pas de deux* was danced by Marlyn Burr and Georges Goviloff – a very showy and exciting dancer. Burr was in sparkling form, I thought, but 'K' noted a tendency to 'jump the beat'.

John Gilpin again danced Witch Boy – the initial shock of the story was blunted, of course, but it still remains a great vehicle for his not always exploited dramatic abilities as well as his excellent technique. Diane Richards took over Anita Landa's part as Barbara. The Dublin premiere of *Boureé Fantasque* a Balanchine ballet to Chabrier music showed the two soloists, Janet Lewis and Jeffrey Kovel in burlesque mood in the witty excerpt. I preferred the prelude, Polonaise and Finale but on the whole another in the 'would like to see' category.

Swan Lake, Act Two, with choreography by Bourmeister (after Ivanov) was given. Irina Borowska seemed to me to be a *terre a terre* dancer. Burr and Richards also danced this role at other performances. Jean-Pierre Alban danced the 'anguished' Prince. There were quite a lot of changes apparent even to me, both for corps and soloists. Benno, the prince's friend is surplus to requirements! Ovations greeting Burr and Gilpin before, during and after the Grand pas from the Nutcracker – Gilpin in exuberant form and Burr sparkling responsively or was it the other way around?

A new production of *Spectre de la Rose* (Fokine/Weber) with sets by Edward Delaney had Dianne Richards as the young girl and Georges Goviloff as the spirit. A very thin lithe dancer, he scarcely seems robust enough, but maybe I have a certain 'type' in my mind and am being unfair.

I was looking forward expectantly to my first performance of *Sherharazade* (Fokine/Rimsky-Korskoff/Bakst), a production revived by Nicholas Beriosoff. It was originally danced in 1910 and must have caused a sensational reaction. Marlyn Burr danced Zobeide. It is a voluptuous, sensuous ballet and the production moved at good pace. The whole company, especially the six odalisques, sultanas and slaves were excellent. Vassili Trunoff danced the Golden Slave. Definitely a 'must-see again'!

The second week commenced with Gilpin and Burr dancing *Napoli* (Bournonville/Helsted/Pauli). Not the whole ballet. Three *divertissments* shows how well Festival Ballet has been able to adapt to and 'adopt' the Bournonville style, which puts so much emphasis on speed and precision. Jeanette Minty in a rather peculiar un-Juliet- like costume, and Louis Godfrey danced the *Romeo and Juliet* (Briansky version) to the Tchaikovsly score and Burr -who has become one of the company's most improved soloists – and Gilpin (alternating with Borowska and Goviloff) danced the *Esmeralda pas de deux* and coda. (Beriosoff/Pugni) and *pas de deux* I hadn't seen before. This was a showy *tour de force piece* and demanded complete confidence and projection, which it got! Encores were called for and were given.

Prince Igor had Vassili Trunoff as the Polovtsian Warrior and Joan Potter the captive slave girl with Anna Delaney dancing the Captive Persian Princess, and Joan Potter the Polovtsian girl. The Borodin music and Fokine Choreography was stirring and, like Sheharazade, moves along at a good pace, driven to the climax. A good performance – how I'd like to have seen the original production!

The Dublin premiere of *The Snow Maiden* (Boumeister/Tchaikovsly) was a fairy story depicting the snowy daughter of Father Frost. Irina Borowska danced the Maiden and was well reviewed by Ulick O'Connor. I thought that a dancer with more elevation would have suited a snow maiden better, and this role was also danced by Diane Richards and Marilyn Burr. I saw Vasilli Trunoff and William Perrie dancing Mizgir and Leil. Jeffrey Kovel danced the Jester. The corps was particularly good and 'K' gives credit to Ballet Mistress and Ballet Master Eileen Ward and Vassili Trunoff. How good it was to see fine dancers such as Trunoff, dancing character roles, which suit him so well. Diane Richards gets kudos from 'K' and from Ulick O'Connor for her Snow Maiden and O'Connor also waxes eloquent, (and expresses my sentiments also) regarding Gilpin, ranking him with Bruhn, Van Dijk, Babilee and Kronstam. Each one was a completely different style of dancer, (all of whom we have been privileged to see, albeit briefly) and of course, Gilpin has given us here in Dublin a continuing chance to witness his technique, dramatic ability and special 'quality.' He returned to the acting stage, and died at a young age, and the death occurred two years later of Anton Dolin. How fortunate we were to have seen them dance so often in Dublin.

20 May 1963. London Ballet, starring Paula Hinton, a very fine sensitive dancer, with guest artist Alexis Rassine, appeared in the Olympia with a company of sixty. Hinton was wonderful as Giselle, especially in the second act, and Rassine danced Albrecht. He had previously danced with the Royal Ballet. The role of Myrtha was danced by Vicki Karras or Anna Pierce and both gave good performances. I have seen many Giselles at this stage, yet two of the most memorable were the Dublin performances of Beryl Goldwyn (Sadlers Wells) and Paula Hinton (London Ballet)

Hoops (choreography Walter Gore) was an Irish premiere – a fairly light- hearted work for seven dancers. The ever- popular *Sylphides* – again Hinton was outstanding, and Rassine suitable noble, gave much pleasure. The corps was particularly light, but the costumes a bit tatty! The full *Nutcracker* was given with, for me, a new discovery, Barrie Wilkinson, as the Prince who alternated with John Bartley, (who, I noted, was an outstanding mechanical soldier in another performance). Deirdre O'Donohoe danced as one of the Snowflakes – (Margot Fonteyn's first role!) I didn't see the Irish premiere of *The Magical Being* or *Shindig* or *Swan Lake* Act Two with Alide Glasbeek as the Swan Queen, with Barrie Wilkinson and Alexis Rassine alternating as the Prince. Michael Pilkington directed the small orchestra.

Just two months after the tribute, Irish National Ballet was disbanded. The last letter from Dame Ninette among Miss Moriarty's papers was written on 15 April 1989:

My dear Joan Denise,
I have just received the sad news about the Arts Council grant. I am so very sorry for you all.
I understand some sort of petition is being got up in this country which will, of course, when it reaches me have my signature.
With all my very best wishes

For the second time, an attempt to establish professional ballet in Ireland had failed. Miss Moriarty may have been inspired by the memory of that first attempt to bring dance to the Abbey Theatre through Ninette de Valois when she chose a late poem by W. B. Yeats as the basis for her last ballet *Sweet Dancer*:

SWEET DANCER[13]

The girl goes dancing there
On the leaf-sown, new-mown, smooth
Grass plot of the garden;
Escaped from a bitter youth,
Escaped out of her crowd,
Or out of her black cloud.
Ah, dancer, ah, sweet dancer!

If strange men come from the house
To lead her away, do not say
That she is happy being crazy;
Lead them gently astray;
Let her finish her dance,
Let her finish her dance.
Ah, dancer, ah, sweet dancer!

To music by Sibelius the ballet was performed by the Cork Ballet Company in the Everyman Theatre Cork, in Crosshaven, in Skibbereen and Tralee in April 1991. Miss Moriarty had not been allowed to finish her dance in the larger domain: she had, however, continued with it in her immediate environment, travelling with her amateur company as far as was possible, encouraging these dancers to choreograph and having them perform their works.

Miss Moriarty created an enduring place for dance in Ireland. Had she been younger when Irish National Ballet was closed down, she would not have rested until it had been restored. May her work be completed.

Reproduction of Yeats poem *Sweet Dancer*

I have a programme of the Ballet Rambert season at the Gaiety (no year or date given) which features *Sweet Dancer* based on a W.B. Yeats poem. Anna Truscott danced, supported by a cast, which included Joanna Banks, Christine Courtney and Marie Lambe, all Irish trained dancers. Kenneth Bannerman danced James in *La Sylphide*, with Cecelia Barrett as the Sylph and Carolyn Fey as the Witch. Joan Denise Moriarty also choreographed a ballet of this name – her last ballet in 1991.

The larger style programme produced by the Gaiety advertises the Merrion School of Ballet, Connollys (Georges St) for Frederick Freed Dancing shoes, and the Desmond Domican Academy of Dancing.

GAIETY

THEATRE

four

The Russians
Are Coming

So are the Corkonians

JULY 29th — AUGUST 10th, 1963

FOR TWO WEEKS ONLY

HE BOLSHOI BALLET

In the Autumn of 1963, there occurred a seismic event – the Bolshoi Ballet made its first appearance in Dublin, at the Gaiety. The glittering array of male and female artists, all of them known world wide since ballet emerged once again from the then U.S.S.R., presented a series of solos, alas, no actual full-length work or even a one act ballet. Of course we were amazed (and prepared to be amazed) by the authority and fluid dancing and acting of Rimma Karelskaya, partnered by Khomutov and we ooh-ed and aah-ed as each of the soloists appeared – one more dramatic than the one before, and all of the highest quality. The climax of the Georgian dance from *Gayane* before the interval had the audience reeling from the impact and the sheer vitality, showmanship and strong techniques, which they somehow manage to adapt to the small stage, when it was obvious that they were accustomed to a much larger one. I particularly loved Raisa Struchkova in her Cinderella variation.

The whole 'audience atmosphere' had changed and becoming as uninhibited as the dancers, flowers were thrown with abandon onto the stage, and bravos and repeated applause interrupted the evening, prolonging it to intoxication point! Even the choreographer's names were now familiar to an audience nurtured by the interest generated by the visiting companies of the 1950s and 1960s, which encouraged us to expand our interest and knowledge.

Gaiety programme of Bolshoi Ballet 1963

Part Two opened with the exquisite Ballet Suite from *Faust* – the various soli bringing an even more vociferous level of applause. Also included was the Spanish Dance from *Swan Lake*. Vladimir Koshelev's Gopek was dynamic as a contrast to the magic of Rimma Karelskaya (those arms, or were they wings?) and to Struchkova and Laupuri brought down the house with the final Waltz. The 'Big' gesture seeming to express the confidence and abandonment to the music was what struck me the most. It was all so effortless and the dancers seemed to enjoy it all as much as the audience, who I think caught the unreservedly positive mood of the audience. A night to remember – the Night the Russians came to Town. Maya Plisetskaya, though listed, did not appear the evening I was there - much to my disappointment. The Radio Eireann Light Orchestra was conduced by Alexis Zhuraytis.

In November 1963, the final Season of Ballet of the year was presented by Patricia Ryan and Joan Denise Moriarty with Belinda Wright and Jelko Yureska at the Olympia, and had a number of Irish Dancers: Gay Brophy, Julia Cotter, Deirdre O'Donohoe, Joahne O'Hara, Joan Wilson, John Bartley, John Cunningham, Domy Reiter and Colin Russell, with guest artist Robert Olup and corps under Geoffrey Davidson. R. E. Light Orchestra played, as did well-known international pianist Charles Lynch.

Cora Boyd with the author and friend at the Ballet.

BOLSHOI'S SECOND PROGRAMME

Last night's Gaiety audience received the second programme of the Bolshoi Ballet with more enthusiasm than discrimination. Of the nine new items, my own humble opinion is that seven were "fillers" —interesting, but not essentially of high quality out of context. The two that were best, to me, at least, were the Struchkova-Lavrovsky *pas de deux* from Prokofiev's "Cinderella," and the Georgian dance from Khachaturian's "Gayane," with Vasilieva, Sitnikov, Simachev, Kashani, Koshelev, and Khomutov. There is also Karelskaya in the Saint-Saens "Dying Swan"—and I still feel its a great pity that this swan wasn't buried with Pavlova. The best of the other new items was a *pas de deux* to Gluck's "Melodie"—the only thing I've seen Cherkasskaya in that didn't irritate me to fury, and this is possibly thanks to Khomutov's partnering. The Georgian dance, like the Spanish *pas de quatre* from "Swan Lake," is given with tremendous verve. Struchkova and Lavrovsky dance the "Cinderella" excerpts with fidelity, rather than inspiration, but Struchkova and Lapauri, in their repeats of last week's Glière "Etude" and Moshkovsky Waltz, strike the same fire that they did in every previous performance—its not only that they do it so magnificently, its how they manage to do it at all! Among the other repeats from last week's amended programme are Kashani's solo from "Gayane," Varlamova's dynamic Gipsy Dance, and Koshelev's Gopak. Above all, however, there is the Pugni "Actaeon and Diane," which, as danced by Lavrovsky and Sorokina, gives one the feeling of seeing a preview of two rising suns of Russian dancing, and inclines this reviewer to state that Sorokina, in a few years time, will be recognised as Ulanova's successor.

Once again, the augmented Radio Eireann Light Orchestra responded magnificently to Algis Zhuraytis, particularly in the Khachaturian.

1963   K.

Fleadh Ceoil

Giselle with Belinda Wright and Yuresha had the Irish dancers in all supporting roles and gave a good account of themselves. Joan Wilson and Robert Olup danced the peasant *pas de deux* and Deirdre O'Donohoe was an excellent Queen Myrtha. *Dark Enchantress,* a wedding story, was well danced by Gabrielle Brophy, Olywyn Acheson, Domy Reiter and John Bartley. Belinda Wright and Jelko Yuresha danced the Grand Pas from *Casse Noisette*– she is my favourite exponent of this role. Joahne O'Hara and John Bartley danced the peasant *pas de deux* from *Giselle. Serefina* (Reiter/Khatchaturian) – a 'relationship' ballet, though short, got across its unique story, with Julia Cotter dancing the role beautifully. *Saudacao a America* and *Dance of the Hours* gave all the dancers a chance to shine and the major work of Joan Denise Moriarty (Hamilton Harty score) was *Prisoners of the Sea* (pianist Charles Lynch). A seal woman assumes a woman's form and leads a fisherman into the sea. His love, Moira, descends to the Kingdom of Manahan and frees the fisherman. The couple plead to be allowed to return to the Aihlinn coast. As this was especially created for the company there is scope for all the dancers, and so rather a lot of characters, but the overall drama surfaced and the production was pleasing. The corps was excellent and the costumes appropriate. A good mainstay, one hoped, of a permanent Irish company. As would also be the case, one hopes, with *Caitlin Boct* (Patricia Ryan/A.J. Potter). It was a mini-history of Ireland with historical figures and artistic muses, Invaders (all male) and judges. Different and definitely Irish! Messrs Guinness and Irish Dunlop and Caltex Ireland Ltd are both acknowledged for their support of this company and its Dublin season.

The Stars of the Bolshoi came once more to the Gaiety in 1965 and enjoyed renewed success, delighting us all with their joyous dancing and strong technique. Rimma Karelskaya and Vladimir Tikhonov danced the adagio from *Swan Lake,* Marius Liepa partnered Ella Dobrochotova in *Spring Waters* and Elena Cherkasskaya and Mickhail Tikhomirnov danced *Romance.* Cherkhassskaya and Begak headed the company in *Walpurgisnacht* – for me the highlight of the evening and a fitting curtain closer. As usual there was a wonderful reception from the enthusiastic Dublin audience.

In 1968 the 'Stars' of the Bolshoi AND of the Kirov came to the Gaiety in March. Once again it was a series of solos and *pas de deux* with the soloists of both companies being new to Dublin. Here indeed was a contrast in styles, although not as easy to discern in the short pieces offered. But even the photographs in the glossy programme showed the difference in arabesque for instance. First soloist of the evening was Alla Osipenko. (Kirov) I was enchanted by the *Swan Lake Adagio* in which she was partnered by Vladilen Semenov, a strong and virile dancer. Jack Cheatle violin, Kathleen Behan, cello and E. Lipa, Piano are credited as accompanying this wonderful adagio. The RTE Orchestra was conducted by Vakhtang Paliashvili. Barbara Potapova danced another adagio *Song of the Forest* with Valery Parsegov, a young dancer who had won the Nijinsky prize in 1964. Quite different in style was a dance simply designated *Pas de deux* choreographed by Galstyan and danced by him and Juliette Kantarian.

Next was Bolshoi star Ludmilla Bogomolova who danced the *Cinderella pas de deux* with Vladimir Nikonov – the Prokofiev music which I was hearing for the first time, *Night Violet* with Inara Abele and Vladimir Gelvan showed us the Kirov style again and the first half ended with the flashy *Esmerelda pas de deux* with Iraida Lukasheva and Valery Nekrasov.

The second half of this well-named programme of 'Stars of the Bolshoi and Kirov Ballets' - artistic director of which was no less a major cosmic star herself - Galina Ulanova – featured Bogomolova and Nikonov again in the grand pas from the *Nutcracker,* (choreography Vainonen), and then the well-loved Raissa Struchkova and Lapauri in *Etude* to Gliere music which went down very well with the audience, especially his solo and the *pas de deux.*

Programme of Grand Divertissements

1 Swan Lake
Adagio   Music : Tchaikovsky
                                          Choreography : Ivanov
Alla Osipenko & Vladilen Semenov
Jack Cheatle, Violin; Kathleen Behan, 'Cello; E. Lipa, Piano

2 Song of the Forest
Adagio   Music : Skorulsky
                                          Choreography : Vronski
Barbara Potapova & Valery Parsegov

3 Pas de deux
                                          Music : Oganesyan
                                          Choreography : Galstyan
Julietta Kantarian & Vilen Galstyan

4 Cinderella
Pas de deux   Music : Prokofiev
                                          Choreography : Zacharov
Ludmilla Bogomolova & Vladimir Nikonov

5 Night Violet
                                          Music : Barison
                                          Choreography : Strod
Inara Abele & Vladimir Gelvan

6 Esmeralda
Pas de deux   Music : Puni
                                          Choreography : Vronski
Iraida Lukasheva & Valery Nekrasov

INTERVAL

7 Nutcracker
Pas de deux   Music : Tchaikovsky
                                          Choreography : Vainonen
Ludmilla Bogomolova & Vladimir Nikonov

8 Étude
                                          Music : Gliere
                                          Choreography : Lapauri
Raissa Struchkova & Alexander Lapauri

9 Kazachok
                                          Music : Ivashenko
                                          Choreography : Segal
Iraida Lukasheva

10 Legend of Love
                                          Music : Melikov
                                          Choreography : Grigorovich
Alla Osipenko & Vladilen Semenov

11 Mountain Dance
from 'Gayane'
                                          Music : Khathaturian
                                          Choreography : Mnatsakanyan
Julietta Kantarian & Vilen Galstyan

12 Gopak
                                          Music : Solovjen-Sedoi
                                          Choreography : Zakharov
Valery Parsegov

13 Waltz
                                          Music : Moskowski
                                          Choreography : Vainonen
Raissa Struchkova & Alexander Lapauri

The Management reserves the right to alter
the programme without notice.

Lighting Equipment by STRAND ELECTRIC LTD.

For the Gaiety Theatre
J. POTTER .... Stage Director
P. JONES .... Stage Manager
S. BURKE .... Chief Electrician
J. EDWARDS .... Press Officer

The public may leave at the end of the performance by all
Exit doors. Persons shall not be permitted to stand or sit in
any of the gangways intersecting the seating, or to sit in any
of the other gangways. (Copy of bye-laws).

The taking of photographs in the auditorium is strictly prohibited.

The central pages of the programme for Kirov and Bolshoi artists 1968

Kazachoc, Legend of Love and Mountain Dance from *Gayana* and a Gopak followed with the soloists from the two schools and the programme ended with the amazing Moskowski waltz with Struchkova and Lapauri, which had so mesmerised us in 1963. There were flashing fireworks and lyricism from this husband and wife duo. The programme was a melange of folksy and fiery items *Flames of Paris*, *Spring Waters* and the *Dance of the Cygnets*.

This was both the beginning and the end of an era. After fifteen wonderful years since the International Ballet came in 1950, an era of visiting companies of varying sizes and budgets, the big Stars had arrived with divertimenti – a forerunner of the arrival of the two great Russian Companies at full strength and with full works. But this was not to be until the 1970s.

BOLSHOI AND KIROV BALLET AT THE GAIETY

By Blanaid O Brolchain

THE PERFORMANCE last night at the Gaiety Theatre described as a Programme of Grand Divertissements by stars of the Bolshoi and Kirov Ballets turned out to be something of a gala occasion, perhaps because Dublin has been so long without ballet, perhaps because the public here are now aware that Russian dancers will always give them good value. Except for a couple of weak spots they had no reason to be disappointed.

This, I believe, is the first time since Pavlova's visit to the Theatre Royal that Dublin has seen members of the Kirov Company which, under its former name of Maryinsky, supplied so many of the dancers with whom Diagheliev first startled Western Europe. If the two principal Kirov dancers who appeared last night are any indication the company has maintained its great tradition, and still specialises in a classically elegant style rather than in the more spectacular and athletic manner of the Bolshoi.

The programme opened with a pas-de-deux from "The Sleeping Beauty" performed with subtlely controlled elegance by Alla Osipenko and Vladilan Semenov of the Kirov. "The Song of the Forest" and "Etude" which followed were danced with a good deal of technical skill but it was wasted on poor choreographic material. The "Cinderella" pas-de-deux showed Ludmilla Bogomolova as a delightful ballerina with mastery of technique and considerable charm, but her partner, Vladimir Nikonov, though strong and spectacular in solo work, showed very little understanding of the great art of partnering. This was shown up even more strongly in the second half of the programme where the same pair performed the "Nutcracker" pas-de-deux (not the "Black Swan" as given in the programme) when surely the writer was not the only person in the audience who recalled nostalgically the perfect performance of the same piece given by Erik Bruhn and Violette Verdy in the Olympia Theatre some years ago.

The prima ballerina of the company, Raissa Struchkova, appeared three times during the programme, dancing with the authority and panache of an acknowledged leader of her art, but she was less satisfactory in the classical "Don Quixote" pas-de-deux than in two familiar pieces in which she was so ably partnered by her husband, Alexandra Lapauri. Both the "Etude" and Waltz have been perfectly worked out by them as a team and it is difficult to imagine either piece being performed by anyone else. The lifts in both are breathtaking, though in the waltz they tend to become a sort of bravura that has very little to do with art, however it may delight the audience.

In the "Don Quixote" pas-de-deux Struchkova was ably partnered not by Labauri as given in the programme but by Vilen Galstian, an energetic dancer with a dashing romantic style.

Two items in the programme which looked unpromising provided surprises each in a very different way. The first was "Night Violet" which looked as if it would be a typical piece of sentimentality but was beautifully and innocently performed by two young dancers, Inara Abele and Vladimir Gelvan. By contrast, in the second half of the programme, Osipenko and Semerov of the Kirov, showed in "Legend of Love" that their artistry was as great in this neurotic modern choreography as ft was in their classical pas-de-deux. Osipenko's supple back and wonderful stretch were in the great Russian tradition and throughout both worked beautifully together to give the maximum in artistic interpretation.

Semerov showed by the expressive use of his hands, how important this can be to give the final touches to an artistic performance.

At the end the audience called for an encore which apparently surprised the artists but was more than deserved.

One of the outstanding features of Russian ballet dancers has always been the quality of their pointe work and all the girls in the company showed the ease and virtuosity expected in this respect. "Kazachok" danced solo by Irzida Lukasheva, though not very interesting otherwise, was a perfect little demonstration of highly skilful pointe work carried off with an ease of manner which quite concealed the years of hard work which had been necessary to produce such proficiency.

It is a pity that we shall never see a Bolshoi or a Kirov company in Dublin performing a full ballet as they do at home, since we have no stage big enough to take even the smallest of their productions. In the meantime we should be grateful for the chance to see even the bits and pieces that have to be strung together to make a night's entertainment of this type. It is only a succession of samples but they are samples of first class work by devoted and well-trained dancers and anyone who is interested in ballet or indeed in art generally should not miss the opportunity.

The music for the evening, though some of it was of poor enough quality, was ably rendered by the Radio Eireann Light Orchestra conducted by Vakhtang Paliashirli.

A review of the Kirov and Bolshoi at the Gaiety in 1968

Autographs were sought at the back lane stage door, Tangiers Lane, but not all the dancers came out this way, and those whom we did get were unfamiliar to us, so that we did not know whose autograph matched whose face and more especially whose signature, as it was in Cyrillic script.

A few years passed before we saw any ballet companies in Dublin. Both my daughters were studying ballet – the elder with Mary Lydon and later the younger one with Deirdre Smith, neé McCartan, contemporary of Doreen Wells of the Royal Ballet. They had studied together at the Bush Davies School, and Deirdre had taught in Belfast before coming to establish her school in Dublin. Teachers and centres multiplied as the 'demand' for authentic training in recognised methods were sought.

AMHARCLANN NA MAINISTREACH
ABBEY THEATRE

Cork Ballet Company

Sunday, 14th November, 1971

At 8.00 p.m.

Programme cover of Cork Ballet 1971

In November 1971 The Cork Ballet Company, who had as patrons Dames Ninette de Valois, Marie Rambert and Alicia Markova, in addition to Cork's Mayor Jane Dowdell, and directed by Joan Denise Moriarty, came to the Abbey Theatre in 1971. Dame Ninette had also come to the Abbey in 1928, at the request of W.B. Yeats to stage the choreography for his *Plays for Dancers* and to found the Abbey Ballet School. The Cork Ballet presented *Comedy Opus for Twenty*. Lavinia Andersen and Anne Walsh danced very well in this work with a Prokofiev score. It was confidently and professionally mounted, as was *Giselle*, which had, as guest stars, Alain Dubreuil and Helen Starr. Hilda Buckley danced Bertha in Act 1 and Lavinia Anderson danced Myrtha in Act Two John O'Donovan danced Hilarion. This was a fine production of a difficult classic and a real pleasure to an Irish company coming into its own.

Le Grand Ballet Classique de France paid a visit to the Olympia and gave a French slant to some old favourites – *Noir et Blanc* (Lifar) a classical ballet marrying academism and neo-classicism, according to the programme notes. Three males in black and three girls in white performed this work with élan and a sort of cerebral approach. Liane Daydé and Georges Goviloff danced and *Interferences*, a short piece concerned with the meaning of life, was danced by Monique Janotta and Jean Golovieff. This company's version of Romeo and Juliet (Tchaikovsky) was danced by the tiny petite Daydé. She did not dance in *Coppélia* which I imagined would have suited her very well, but *Swanhilda* was danced by Jacqueline de Min, a very classical looking dancer. The second programme was *Edyades* (Creation) *Le Corsaire pas de deux*, and *Idylle* all preceded *Coppélia* with the same cast as before. A very comprehensive programme booklet included a history of French traditions and a poem on the company's world tour. We were happy that they came to Dublin.

They were followed in 1972 by Tanz Forum, (Cologne) who came to the Abbey with a very international cast of young dancers presenting two uncompromisingly modern programmes, concluding each with a performance of the *Green Table*, the third time this stark anti-war ballet had been seen in Dublin. Creation Boutique advertised full page on the back cover of the programme and a large advertisement for Carrokeel Irish wolfhounds was also prominent.

Also in 1972 The Cork Ballet came to celebrate it 25th season in existence at the Gaiety in Dublin. They mounted the full-length *Swan Lake* with Sandra Conley (of the Royal Ballet) dancing Odette/Odile partnered by Alain Dubreuil and with Mary Hanf (San Francisco Ballet). This was a major triumph for the company, as it had been many years since we had seen the full ballet. The company rose magnificently to the occasion.

By now, twenty years had elapsed since my first performance, beginning with the gloriously classical International Ballet and ending with the modern Tanz forum, and the Cork Ballet Company.

In 1973 the New London Ballet appeared at the Abbey. There were some familiar names: Prokovsky, Richards, Elaine McDonald. Galina Samsova had been associated with Joan Denise Moriarty in one of her productions. And Joan Denise Moriarty produced a delightful *Nutcracker* and *The Golden Bells of Ko* at the Gaiety in 1973. I remember my girls being absolutely delighted with these productions and begging to be brought again. They had to wait until the following year.

In 1974 the Cork company was back again with *Giselle*, and *Full Moon for the Bride*. Once again, a ballet with an Irish theme. Joan Denise Moriarty and A.J. Potter produced the classic. Patricia Dillon danced the Bride (Bridin) and Shaun Higgins the Bridegroom. The Strawboys, masked, arrive near midnight each now being allowed to dance with the bride. May, being the month of the Little People, the faeries try to lure the bride away.

Irish Ballet Teacher, Deirdre Smith, seen here as a student

Giselle, too, is full of mystery and supernatural power. In Act 1 Joahne O'Hara as principal of the company danced Giselle, the peasant girl. Patrick Hurde danced the hero Albrecht and danced his solo well but was more at ease in Act Two. Joahne O'Hara was very moving as Giselle, one of the most demanding roles in all of classical ballet and for her it was a personal triumph. Lavinia Anderson gave a good interpretation of Myrtha, also a difficult role. Jim O'Connell was a good believable Hilarion in Act.1. A good night for Irish Ballet.

As part of the Dublin Theatre Festival in October 1978, the Irish Ballet Company gave a season at the Olympia presenting *Playboy of the Western World* accompanied by The Chieftains – a wonderful partnership. Anna Donovan danced Pegeen and Sean Cunningham Christy Mahon, in this Synge drama. A very convoluted tale, it takes all the company's acting power to convey this story to those who are not familiar with it. It was an ambitious ballet and a welcome major work for the company. Not sure whether I enjoyed it, but I admire the production of it.

In 1978 Joan Denise Moriarty, as Artistic Director, presented a varied programme at the Abbey, offering a semi-abstract ballet with Beck choreography for ten dancers. Bournonville's *Flower Festival* needs a very particular style. Tricia Hirch and Stephen Rochford gave a creditable performance. *Othello* (Lizst/Darnell) had a well-known theme requiring no imagination, so one could enjoy the dancing of Sean Cunningham and Joanna Banks as Emilia and a cast of five dancers. *Shadow Reach* had a more complicated theme and probably needs several viewings. Kathleen Smith was strong as the Governess.

The second week offered *Konservatoriet* – another Bournonville ballet. Ric Able, Kathleen McInerney and Victoria Lee did a good job in this vignette depicting the progress of the boy Bournonville when he was sent to Paris to study with Vestris. *Concerto Grosso* (Handel) formerly given by Festival Ballet was a ballet which suited the company well and they obviously enjoyed dancing it. *Chariots of Fire* (Christon/Reiter) tells the rather complicated story of Phaedre, giving plenty of scope for dramatic dancing from Kathleen Smith and Richard Collins, Ric Abel and Anna Donovan. *The Devil to Pay*, with Moriarty / O'Riada, had an Irish theme and Ceolteoiri Cualann performed the music. Sean Cunningham, Anna Donovan, Carol Burgess and Kathleen McInerney danced in this ballet, which was mounted for their fifth birthday – a real triumph for a professional Irish company.

In 1981 I attended a performance of *The Tain*, Joan Denise Moriarty's second full-length work for the Dublin Theatre Festival, with sets by Patrick Murray and a score by Aloys Fleischmann, in which the RTE Concert Orchestra was conducted by Proisnsias O'Duinn. I remember in particular Roger Wade, Sean Cunningham and Anna Donovan.

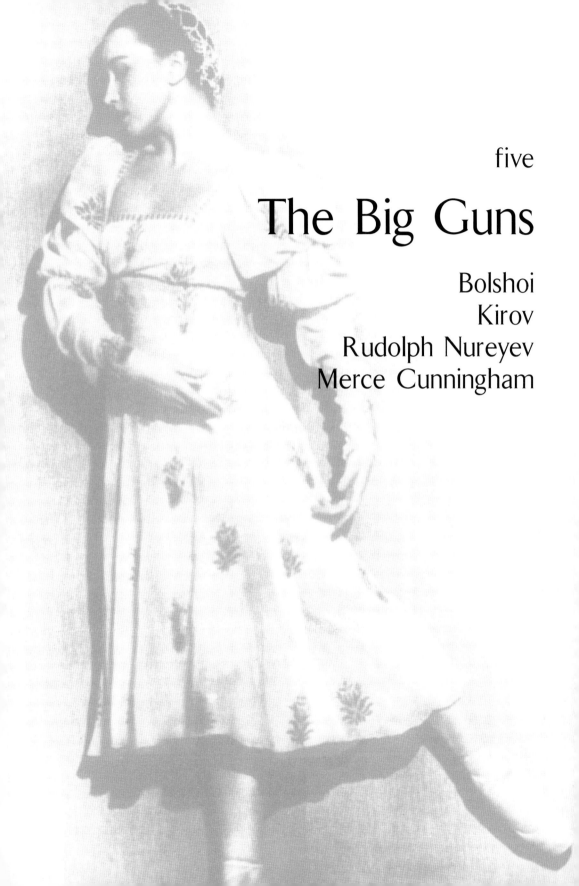

five

The Big Guns

Bolshoi
Kirov
Rudolph Nureyev
Merce Cunningham

During the twenty years and more since 1981 we had visits of various Russian or Russian Republics-based companies, the most major of which was the never-to-be –forgotten visit of the full Bolshoi Company in 1986, which produced full length works at the Royal Dublin Society's Simmonscourt Pavilion. Prudential Life sponsored this major event and a large glossy programme (photos by Snowdon) was on sale at a price much in excess of the modest Gaiety and Olympia programmes of old.

Dublin was their first venue prior to a tour of Britain and lists thirty-six principals and a company of one hundred. The Irish Ballet Orchestra, (Symphony Orchestra – leader Alan Smale) was conducted by Alexander Kopylov Alexander Lavrenyuk. The Artistic Director was Yuri Grigorovitch – a former dancer with the company.

I went to the first very special performance by myself and the next day. I was accompanied by my two daughters. I remember we drank champagne 'by the neck' to celebrate! This was the first time that I had heard an audience requested to switch off digital watches - in addition to a plea to refrain from coughing! Well, this was the Big Time and we awaited the parting of the velvet curtains, as opposed to 'curtain up' in the smaller theatres. The RDS was not ideal but such was the theatricality of the dancers and the good sound produced by the orchestra, that it was possible, with a little effort, to imagine oneself in a Russian theatre.

The ballet was one of the lovliest *Sylphides* I have ever seen, with Bessmertnova (Natalya) Yuri Vasyuchenko, Nina Ananiashvili, Nina Semizorova and Bessmertnova (Tatyana) and it was indeed a magical performance. Natalya Bessmertnova was truly outstanding amongst the very superior cast and it was a beautiful experience.

After an interval, which helped to bring me back to the RDS surroundings, we had a series of divertissements ranging from dances from *Coppélia* to *The Golden Age*. Showpiece after showpiece followed. Surely this was a second Golden Age for Dublin. The excitement that this visit generated, especially for a further generation of Irish dancers and teachers, showed that this was not merely an event on the theatrical social calendar. Of course the Bolshoi was a must-see for Dublin theatre- goers and it also generated an appreciation amongst an audience new to the wonderful world of ballet. Far from the days of queuing for the gallery, this was an expensive outing booked well in advance, because, in the words of the advertisement for the current L'Oreal products:'They're Worth It!' After the second interval, there was the exciting *Spartacus* – known to ballet aficionados through *Dancing Times* and photographs – which had long been in the company's repertoire, with Khachaturian score and Grigorovitch choreography. The wonderful Natalya Bessmertnova was dancing again as Phrygia, wife of Spartacus. Listed amongst the Ballet Masters/Repetiteurs were Nikolai Simachov, Raissa Struckhova, so beloved of Dublin audiences in 1963/8, and Galina Ulanova – the legendary *'prima ballerina assoluta'* was a ballet 'coach' to the leading ballerinas.

Galina Ulanova

I noted that the performance on Saturday evening was scheduled to end at 10.45 pm and that it didn't actually finish till 11.15 p.m. Ulanova and the Director were persuaded on stage to great acclaim- wild enthusiastic acclaim, in fact. Later I was fortunate enough to meet her and the Director briefly and they graciously signed my precious little book, as did many of the principals. The programme was the same as at the matinee, but with Maria Bylova dancing Phrigia, and the climax of the evening was the *pas de deux* from Le Corsaire, with Lyudmila Semenyaka and Andris Liepa, son of Maris.

In 1988 Dublin celebrated its Millenium (Dublin is Great in '88) and as part of that celebration, the fabled Kirov Ballet of St. Petersburg and the Imperial Court (for a time named the Maryinsky) appeared, again at the RDS sponsored by American Express. It was an equally large company of twenty-two principals under the direction of Oleg Vinogradov for a week's season. The realisation that we were probably seeing the best of the very best of the old Imperial School's present products was enhanced by the sumptuous souvenir programme, given the history of Maryinsky and its past and present principals.

Ciara Batt and Karina Batt in 1969

The Irish Ballet Orchestra, again accompanied, conducted by Viktor Federov and Dzhemal Dalgat. Once again I managed to get to three performances, seeing the Act Three of *La Bayadere*, with its famous ensemble for the corps. After the interval there was a variety of classical pieces, including *Les Papillon*, (choreography by Marie Taglioni!), the *Pas de Six* from *Esmerelda* and *Pas de Six* from *La Vivindiere*. The third part of the programme was a selection from *Paquita* showing the strength of the female dancers. Olga Chenchikova was partnered by Konstantin Zaklinsky.

On Saturday they presented a full *Swan Lake* – a rare treat to see a fully mounted production of a major classic, by such a historic company. Lyubov Kunakova danced Odette/Odile with wonderful authority and poignancy, and she was partnered by Marat Daykayev. Yuri Fateyev, as the Jester, was outstanding. All the dancers seem to dance with a special authority – not showy, unless required, sure in technique, being merely tools of the trade and with great emphasis on interpretation and fluency of movement.

Ciara Batt and Karina Batt at the pre-Bolshoi event in 1989.

I will dwell in detail about these major visits, as so many will have their own memories. It was the Golden Age for new balletomanes, and it could hardly have been more golden.

In 1989, Ryanair sponsored a return visit by the Bolshoi Ballet, which once again, performed *Spartacus* and a *Ballet Spectacular*. Natalya Bessmertnova again danced Phrygia and the exciting Irek Mukhamedov danced Spartacus. The lovely Maria Bylova was Aegina. In the *Spectacular Giselle* Act Two was given with Lyudmila Sememyaka and Irek Mukhamedov. Nina Ananiashvili was Myrtha. She also danced the Nutcracker *pas de deux* with Aleksei Fadeyechev. *Raymonda* Act Three featured practically all the dancers, in a spectacular finale indeed!

Bolshoi Ballet at Point Depot

By Carolyn Swift

THE BOLSHOI may be criticised on the grounds that its repertoire is hardly innovative, but it is impossible not to be bowled over by its superb soloists, and they are seen at their brilliant best in the *divertissements* of the last two sections of their first programme, since the third act of "Raymonda", like the last act of all classical ballets, is really *divertissements* also.

This Pashkova and Petipa work, rarely danced in the West, ends with the wedding of Raymona and her crusader, Jean de Brienne, as occasion for the usual Mazurka and Hungarian and Classical dances, all brilliantly costumed and finely presented around the diminutive prima ballerina Natalya Bessmertnova and Yuri Vasyuchenko, his considerable height making even the huge new stage of the Point Depot barely big enough to contain his *grand jetés*.

As for the middle section of acknowledged *divertissements*, when the Bolshoi bills a *pas de deux* the jewelled performances are not wrenched from their brilliant settings, but presented as the excerpts are danced when the works are given in full. Thus it is only Lyudmila Semenyaka's "Dying Swan", surely as birdlike and moving as ever Pavlova was, and Alla Mikhalchenko and Irek Mukhamedov's "le Corsaire" *pas de deux*, with Mikhalchenko tossing off *fouettés* as casually as a schoolgirl skipping and Mukhamedov's incredible leaps and double turns that are without supporting soloists or *corps*.

In the *pas de deux* from "The Nutcracker", for instance, Nina Ananiashvili's scintillating Sugar Plum Fairy variations are preceded by a stage full of splendid characters — not assorted sweets as in the West, but the personages of a grand court — and, although Artistic Director Yuri Grigorovich's version is different from the one with which we are familiar, she still has the famous fish dive, ably partnered by Alexsei Fadeychev.

New to me was Grigorovich's "The Legend of Love" to music by Arif Melikov, of which we were given the Adagio. An oriental tale with appropriately odalisque poses and exotic lifts, this was well performed by Maria Bylova and Yuri Vasyuchenko.

For Grigorovich's modern work "The Golden Age", we had the restaurant and its guests for backing, with Gediminas Taranda as the dashing and dangerous bandit leader and Bessmertnova as his brilliant dancing partner, in their cabaret tango, while the Grand Pas from "Don Quixote" had Nina Semizorova doing pinpoint *fouetés* that could have been placed on a 10p piece, with Alexander Vetrov showing equal virtuosity, with saucy variations from Elena Borisova dn Nina Speranskaya.

The romantic style of Act 2 of "Giselle", with which the first programme opens, is not that which suits this company best, yet I have never seen a performance so strongly evocative of the 19th century, continually calling to mind lithographs of the earliest productions. Nor have I ever seen an Albrecht as well able as Irek Mukhamedov to convince us both that he is dying from exhaustion while performing leaps an Olympic athlete might envy and that his Giselle is an insubstantial ghost while raising her high above his head. Without Act One, it is impossible for the Giselle to portray the innocent, vivacious and loving girl whose tragic betrayal has caused her madness and suicide, but Semenyaka manages to hint at the girl she was before she became a ghost, while Ananiashvili, who alternates the role with her was last night a brilliant myrtha, authoritative and proudly beautiful.

Alexander Kopylov conducted the Ballet orchestra, led by Audrey Collins at a tempo of which the composers would all have approved, since the dancers' fine techniques enabled them to hold their *pointes* for as long as required. Do not miss the chance to see this wonderful company, or Grigorovich's best full-length work "Spartacus" at the weekend.

Philippe Cassard and Takács Quartet

By Michael Dervan

String Quartet in C K465 (Dissonance)	Mozart
String Quartet in A flat Op 105	Dvorak
Piano Quintet	Brahms

THE Takács String Quartet at their best are a chamber music ensemble without peer, especially in the music of their compatriot, Bartók. For their 58th concert in Ireland, given at the Royal Hospital, Kilmainham, yesterday, they cast Bartók aside and settled for other staples from their repertoire — Mozart, Dvorak and Brahms. Oddly enough, these players seem to have been heard here more frequently in the quintets of Brahms than in

Times review of the Bolshoi at the point in 1989

Prudential Life presents

THE BOLSHOI BALLET

at the Royal Dublin Society, Simmonscourt

Director: **Stanislav Lushin**

Artistic Director and Chief Choreographer: **Yuri Grigorovich**

Designer: **Simon Virsaladze**

DIVERTISSEMENT PROGRAMME I

Conductor: **Alexander Lavrenyuk**

The Irish Ballet Orchestra
Leader: **Alan Smale**

Saturday 19 July 1986
Matinée

PHOTOGRAPHS
All ballet photographs incorporated in advertisements in the Souvenir Programme have been shot on 3M 640T film, photographed by Vladimir Prebobin or Alexandra Stone.

PLEASE NOTE
Would you please try to restrain coughing and the normal breaks in the performance. A more modern distraction than the cough is the chiming digital watch, both audience and performers would appreciate these being turned off or suppressed.
Persons shall not be permitted to stand or sit in any of the gangways. If standing shall be permitted in the gangways, at the sides and rear of the seating, it shall be limited to the numbers exhibited in those positions.
The taking of photographs is not permitted. Members of the public are reminded that no camera, tape recorder, other type of recording apparatus, food or drink may be brought into the auditorium. It is illegal to record any performances or part thereof unless prior arrangements have been made with the Director and the concert promoter concerned.
No photography is allowed in the auditorium.
No smoking in the auditorium.

The Bolshoi Ballet poster from the 1986 visit to the RDS, Dublin.

Programme front cover from the Kirov Ballet's visit to Dublin in 1990

The Kirov Ballet poster from the 1990 visit to the Point Theatre, Dublin.

In 1990 the Kirov (formerly the Maryinsky) was back again, at the Point Theatre, again sponsored by Ryanair. This time there were more new Principals and soloists for a ten- day season in which they mounted a full length *Le Corsaire* and *Swan Lake*. As with the Bolshoi, we see the male dancers in equally demanding dancing roles, not only as a partner. Their love of dancing and the virility of performance was evident in their varied Russo/Tatar/Slovak backgrounds and was exhilarating and exciting, moving Dublin audiences to new expressions of appreciation. In *Le Corsaire*, Yevgeny Neff and Kiril Melnikov and Konstantin Zaklinsky as Ali, made me realise that we were seeing the equals in technique of Rudolf Nureyev. In fact Zaklinsky was not unlike Nureyev in appearance and his *joie de vivre* as assurance in his dancing is a joy. How often had I regretted that I had not been able to see this famed dancer, about whom so much has been written – the Nijinsky of his age? Or, more probably, the Nureyev of All Seasons!

In fact, I did get my wish to see Nureyev on stage in 1990 – as Dr. Coppelius with the Cleveland San Jose Ballet Company. Obviously the main emphasis was on his mime, dance opportunities being limited. What a boost it must have been for this company, to have such an artist, and what an experience for Melissa Mitchell and Oliver Nunoz to dance on the same stage as the maestro. I met him briefly, in his black beret, after the performance and to have spoken to him and to have his signature next to Dame Margot's and to see him on a Dublin stage (The Point) was indeed a privilege. No Irish ancestry in his Asiatic Mongol, Moslem Tartar background! However, he had recorded a disc in London in 1975 with Miceal MacLiammoir, as the Soldier in Stravinsky's *The Soldier's Tale*.

I often regret not having seen him in performance in London, especially in those early days when he formed that unique partnership with Margot Fonteyn, as exemplified by the ballet *Marguerite and Armand*. Those were the years when the children were small, and it simply would not have entered my head to 'take off' for a couple of days for a theatrical performance. Those were the days of financial constraints for most people and summer holidays were firmly fixed. I do remember being amazed at hearing of someone who had 'taken off' to go and hear Maria Callas sing. How I wish now that I had somehow contrived to go and see that famous partnership dance! Rudolph Nureyev was born on St. Patrick's Day in 1938 on a train en route to Vladivostock, and he died on 6 January 1993. He is buried in the Russian Orthodox Cemetery south of Paris.

Merce Cunningham's Company appeared at the Abbey on the opening night of the International Dance Festival of Ireland in 2002, as far as I know the only time that his company has visited Ireland. The costumes and décor for *Summerspace* were striking yet blending and the dance, characteristic of Cunningham's choreographic style. Sort of hypnotic! 'Biped' was equally compelling, quite a shock to the system. The dancers were still performing as the curtain was lowered.

Since then various Russian Companies and touring sections of companies have brought full- length productions of *Swan Lake* and the *Nutcracker* (Moscow City Ballet). Moscow Festival Ballet mounted *Divertissements*, and Act Two of *Giselle* and *The Sleeping Princess*. Russian Ballet Fireworks (National Concert Hall), and the Perm State Ballet stars have also danced at NCH, and at The Point, both *Romeo and Juliet* (Prokovief) and *Cinderella* have had full-length performances in recent times, both very exciting, especially *Romeo and Juliet*.

The Russian State Ballet mounted *Swan Lake* and *The Nutcracker* at the Point in December 2005. Odette/Odile was danced by Liudmila Konovalova. As I was quite near to the stage I was able to witness up close not only her formidable technique, but also her expressive interpretation. She seemed to me to be very young (especially when I met her very briefly after the performance) but I note that she is listed as 'prima ballerina'. Her performance will mature even more in future years, I feel sure, and she will merit her prestige title for a long time to come. Her Prince was Yury Vyskubenko and Viraly Manin was a believable Jester, also possessing a strong technique and a spirit of fun.

PROGRAMME

THE NATIONAL ANTHEM.

1. Valse : **A Thousand and One Nights.** Strauss.
   MYRTLE LAMKIN, OLGA MOHAN, MARY LYDON.

2. **Red Riding Hood :**
   DEIRDRE HODGINS.

3. Cantata for Alto, Choir and Orchestra :
   "Christmas Eve." Gade (Op. 40).
   (Alto Soloist : MAURA O'REILLY).

4. Quintette for Clarinet and Strings :
   "A Major." Mozart.

   Clarinet : MR. J. P. KELLY.
   Violin : MISS BLOOM POLLOCK.
   do. MISS ELLARD.
   Viola : MRS. C. P. HARDING.
   'Cello : MISS J. McLOUGHLIN.

5. Ballet : **"Where the Brook and River meet.'**

   Story & Choreography : GERVAISE MATHEWS.
   Music : C. O'DONNELL SWEENEY.
   Lighting : MICHAEL MATHEWS.

   "Standing with reluctant feet
   Where the brook and river meet,
   Womanhood and childhood fleet."
   (Longfellow.)

   STORY :

   The girl is passing from her carefree, thoughtless childhood into the world of grown people. She experiences, for the first time, doubts, which torment and sway her. Love comes, but, at first, she does not understand it. Then, fears, unseen, terrify her ; but when joy appears she realises that she is now consciously aware of it. She is almost crushed by the horror of hate, but when love returns to comfort her she accepts it.

   She is surrounded by these emotions of the adult world, but now they hold no mystery for her—she is a woman.

   Musical Director : C. O'DONNELL SWEENEY, MUS. B. N.U.I.

CAST :

The Girls : GERVAISE MATHEWS, MYRTLE LAMBKIN.
Doubts : OLGA MOHAN, DOREEN RYAN.
Love : TONY BAILEY.
Fears : ELINOR MATHEWS, AVERIL GRANEY.
Joy : MARY LYDON.
Hate : MICHAEL MATHEWS.

: INTERVAL :

6. (a) **"Minuet" :** Boccherini.
   OLGA MOHAN.

   (b) **"The Swan" :** Saint-Saens.
   AVERIL GRANEY.

7. An unfinished opera :
   "Loreley." Mendelssohn (Op. 98).
   (Soprano, Choir and Orchestra).

   (a) **"Ave Maria."**
   (b) **"Vintage Song."**
   (c) **Finale Act I.**

   (Soprano Soloist : PEGGY O'REGAN).

8. Ballet : Excerpt from the **"Swan Lake."** Tchaikowsky.
   "The Four Little Swans."
   AVERIL GRANEY, OLGA MOHAN, MARY LYDON, MYRTLE LAMBKIN.

9. Ballet : **"Waltzes from Vienna."** Strauss.
   Soloists : MARY LYDON and AVERIL GRANEY.
   MYRTLE LAMBKIN.
   OLGA MOHAN.
   DOREEN RYAN.

   THE ABBEY SCHOOL OF BALLET.
   Directed by MURIEL CUFFE.

This programme is subject to alteration without notice.

Central Pages of Dun Laoghaire Choral & Orchestral Society and Abbey School of Ballets' 1944 production

Ireland's own Perm trained dancer, Monica Loughman, a pupil of Marie Cole in Dublin, has toured with the Perm Ballet and has danced at the National Concert Hall. I was fortunate to see her debut in *Giselle* at the Point. She has also danced in Cork and at other venues in Ireland. Monica has written book about her time in Perm and it gives a realistic account of her years there and the hardships and difficulties she and the other Irish students had to overcome. Not all managed to do this, and Monica and her fellow students who stayed the course graduated with great honour and have brought their art to Ireland, where Monica has danced major roles with great distinction. She had also appeared on television and has been involved in the production of a series of class –to-performance programmes, with Alan Foley. This is now available on DVD and is enjoying great success. Monica has recently opened a new school in which students are taught a more Russian - styled syllabus. A movie telling her life story is also soon to be in production.

It is all a very different scene since the 1950s - half a century ago. Short stints in large venues are the norm nowadays. The St. Petersburg Ballet has appeared in both Dublin and Belfast. The Point Theatre and at the NCH have been joined by The

Above: Anne Maher of Ballet Ireland

Right: Irish Times review of Perm State Ballet by Carolyn Swift at the Pavilion in Dun Laoghaire

Far right: Times review of Giselle 2003

Opposite: Monica Loughman as Giselle, from her book *Irish Ballerina*

Perm State Ballet of Russia 2001
Pavilion, Dún Laoghaire

ON Sunday night, the Perm State Ballet of Russia was more-than-a-little cramped on the stage of the Pavilion, Dún Laoghaire, which is like a postage stamp compared with the stage of the Opera House in Perm, but it was a privilege to see this superb company from so close. Every tiny detail of technique and expression was visible, yet all was perfection in a company that, unlike many in Russia, still retains all of *Giselle's* the beautiful mime, making the romantic story of this 1841 Coralli and Perrot ballet easy to follow.

Elena Kulagina was wonderful as the shy, dance-loving peasant betrayed into madness and death in Act 1, and the insubstantial ghost she becomes in Act 2, while Roman Geer convincingly acted the false, and later contrite, lover while dancing and partnering superbly. Radiy Miniakhmetov was splendid as the jealous gamekeeper who exposes the deception and Natalia Moiseeva and Sergei Mershin gave a classic rendering of the Act 1 *pas de deux*. Yulia Mashkina was a commanding Queen of the Wilis, while her assistants Zulma and Moyna were beautifully danced by Rimma Siraeva and Monica Loughman.

But the proof of quality of this outstanding company was the perfect grace and unity of the *corps de ballet*, rivalled only by the Kirov, from which Perm partly derives. Sets and costumes (by T. Bruny and E. Leschinsky) were enchanting, though Act 2 seemed less wooded than the plot would suggest, and Adolphe Adam's score was excellently played, even though recorded. This was *Giselle* at its best.

Carolyn Swift

Reviews

Giselle
The Point, Dublin

HELEN MEANY

Regimes and governments in Russia may fall and change but one certainty endures; that the Russian State Ballet will venture from its base inside the Kremlin to bring the classical repertoire to audiences around the world. This is the fifth visit to Dublin by this versatile touring company, founded in 1979, which has attracted dancers from the Bolshoi, Kirov and Stanislavski ensembles. This year the Irish ballerina, Monica Loughman, who trained with Perm State Ballet, joins them as guest soloist in the title role of *Giselle*.

The high Romanticism of *Giselle* is a showcase for the company's technical excellence: the vivid upper-body expression, the precision of the dancers' line, turn-out and elevation, and, in the second act, the illusion of utter weightlessness. A simple narrative of betrayed love is expanded to create a display of virtuosity. The first act, set in an idealised medieval German village, is crammed with a succession of *divertissements*, establishing the apparently immutable social hierarchies. The peasants are a cheerful lot, none more so than Giselle, who has fallen in love with Albrecht (Andrey Joukov), unaware that he is a prince in disguise. His unmasking introduces the high point of the first act, as Giselle, unhinged by grief, dances to death.

The ethereal beauty of the second "white" act, set in the realm of the dead, embodies the studied perfection of Romantic ballet. Perrot's choreography from 1841 - reconstituted here by the company's artistic director, Vyacheslav Gordeev - significantly developed the dramatic possibilities of dance. The *corps de ballet* participate fully in the drama as Wilis, the spirits of women who have been wronged by men. As she protects Albrecht from their vengeful intentions, Giselle is required to express depths of pain and love, which Loughman captures eloquently.

By dancing with him until daybreak she saves his life; this exquisite *pas de deux*, in which the disembodied Giselle seems to slip through Albrecht's arms, gliding *en pointe*, transforms the problematic notion of female sacrifice into a more universal expression of forgiveness and transcendence. One briefly awkward landing between these two superb dancers was a reminder that, contrary to appearances, they are in fact human.

♦ *Returns to the Point tomorrow*

Paul Weller
Olympia Theatre, Dublin

Helix as a new venue. Irish National Ballet and Dublin City Ballet, two professional companies, flourished for a time, but like many another ventures, foundered for lack of official subsidy.

However, Ballet Ireland (Artistic Directors Anne Maher and Gunther Falusy) continues to give performances in small theatres all over Ireland. Anne studied with Myrtle Lambkin until, at the age of sixteen, she went to teach in Cork for Joan Denise Moriarty. She returned to dance professionally with Dublin City Ballet and subsequently went to live in Munich where she developed ballet in that city with Gunther Falusy, before returning to Ireland where they founded, and are co-directors, of Ballet Ireland. They present ballet all over the country and in many theatres in Dublin and environs. The recent *Red Shoes* programme – homage to Diaghilev –has been seen at many venues, the premiere being held at the National Concert Hall. A 'new take' on *Spectre de la Rose* and *L'Après-midi d'un Faune* and *Sacre du Printemps* were mounted, in addition to *Red Shoes* and the more classical pieces.

Recently I came across a Programme dating from 1944 in which Myrtle Lambkin, Mary Lydon and Olga Mohan danced, being members of the Abbey School of

Ballet. The programme itself had advertisements for the original Jury's Hotel, then situated on College Green, John Neiland & Son, Victuallers, Arthur Forster, First class Hairdresser and Wigmaker, Potter's College, Dun Laoghaire, Lynch & O'Brien, Wine Merchants and Walters – the latter two still in business in Dun Laoghaire. Dr. H. Mackey, Dr. T. M. Corbet and Mr. Justice McCarthy were President and Vice Presidents of the Society. Programme price: 6d.

Oscar Theatre Ballet, Director Louis O'Sullivan, presented a short season in the Pavilion Cinema in Dun Laoghaire in the 1970s. Nowadays ballet is accessible to all, at the Civic Theatre, Tallaght, and The Moat Theatre, Naas, and the Mermaid Theatre in Bray to name just a very few, and of course the Project has long been a pioneer of dance, classical and modern. Dance Theatre of Ireland, whose headquarters at Dun Laoghaire had the privilege of welcoming President McAleese to their official opening, is under the direction of Loretta Yurick and Robert Connor, and mounts productions at the Pavilion Theatre. Diversions, an exciting company from Wales, and Independent Ballet of Wales regularly visit the Pavilion Theatre in Dun Laoghaire and indeed soloists from the Perm Ballet staged *Giselle* there, in which Monica Loughman also danced.

This book is not intended to be a definitive history of ballet in Dublin, but to record my own treasured memories. My 'brief' has been to highlight the ballet scene in Dublin city, especially in the Fifties and Sixties, from a fan's point of view and to try to recapture for readers that very special time of visiting companies that enthralled and educated us. We should all be so grateful to the managements of the Gaiety and the Olympia, who led us into the second 'era' still going forward from strength to strength, and delighting us anew in the Nouvelle Golden Age.

Postcript

I have been lucky to have seen many ballet performances abroad – my first experience being, as already described at London's Covent Garden, where I subsequently saw many more ballets over the years, including Darcey Bussell's debut as Cinderella. I've seen *The Nutcracker* at Shaftesbury Avenue and at the old Vic Wells theatre. I saw Western Theatre Ballet in Glasgow. It was tremendous to see the Bolshoi in Moscow and dancers of the Maly (Mahly) Theatre in St. Petersburg. The Kirov was abroad at the time, but I was given a special tour of the theatre. I was baffled by the system of getting into the Maly theatre. I got a ticket, but my companions were refused- even when proffering the admittance in various currencies! When I took my place in a Box, there was room for several more people! The Russian audience was quite talkative during the performance discussing, out loud, various aspects of the performance. They were also noisy in acclaiming solos, mid-ballet. Since the ballet was *Giselle*, I was certainly surprised. I had no way of knowing from the Russian programme in Cyrillic script the soloist who was dancing the lead, (E. H. Estyeeva) but she was young, beautiful and a most believable Giselle – definitely in my top three. Later, under the influence of neat vodka, I am assured I donned the ballet slippers that I had bought in the foyer of the theatre, and danced on the table (with no ribbons!).

I've been fortunate to see ballet in great Opera Houses in Europe in Budapest; Copenhagen (a Balanchine programme); the *Sleeping Princess* in the Rome Opera House; in Vienna; in Amsterdam; The Lincoln Centre in New York; the Wang Centre in Boston; the Moisseiev Ballet Company in Paris and a Gala Season of the Bolshoi in the Albert Hall. I've been many times to Covent Garden and to the Festival Hall. The English National ballet dedicated their performance of *The Nutcracker* there in 1993 to the memory of Nureyev, whose death had just been announced that day. I also saw Nutcracker performed in Belfast and at the Civic Theatre in Tallaght! Not to mention Matthew Bourne's 'alternative' Nutcracker at Sadlers Wells. Missed his alternative *Swan Lake*, though! I've also seen Japanese dancing during a performance at the Kabuki Theatre in Tokyo. Recently I attended a performance in Stockholm's splendid Opera House with my friend Inger, of three splendidly danced ballets, accompanied by a full Orchestra, solo clarinet and solo pianist. Stockholm has a unique museum – the world's first museum of the Dance, opened in 1999, depicting the history of the dance from its earliest beginnings to the present time.

It is interesting to note, that although technically strengthened, ballet slippers appear to be the same nowadays as they always were. But the tutu has ranged from the soft, light, wide and 'flowing' variety that Pavlova wore, to the short stiff, and 'puffy' upward pointing style that prevailed in the 60's and back again to the softer 'spreading' from the basque in a 'downward' direction that one sees nowadays. Fashions change even in ballet design!

Muly = the name for front cover of Russian (Tolstoy) State Ballet
Company in 1989

Above: Rudolf Nureyev and Raymond Rodriguez at rehearsals during their visit to Dublin in 1990

Opposite above: Waiting for curtain up at the Gaiety – Olive Montgomery, Helen Delahunty, Valerie Schomers and Stephanie Batt

Opposite below: The Gaiety stage, Dublin

The author attending the class of Deirdre O'Neill, at the Dance Theatre of Ireland in 2006

Above and below: Autographs obtained by the author – Rudolph Nureyev and Margot Fonteyn

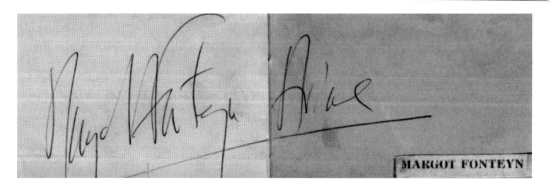

Three stars of the Bolshoi and the Kirov Ballet dance with students of the Ballet School, Ranelagh, 1968 (The Sunday Press)

The method of preserving, and thus reviving a ballet is aided in this technical age by video and DVD recording expertise. This replaces and /or augments the Benesh and Labanotation methods and even earlier methods, so valuable in their day. Nijinsky, too, had his own method of recording choreography. Of course the dancers themselves are the custodians of the choreographer's art.

I hope readers have enjoyed this journey through the past and that it has brought back happy memories. I have not listed every ballet performed and readers will be able to fill gaps for themselves. Many of them will have seen performances that I have missed.

I dedicate this little 'history' to all those wonderful companies, their Directors and Sponsors, from abroad or from our own shores that have come, and are still coming, to enchant us in Dublin. It is also dedicated to the teachers of ballet in Ireland. Long may they continue to instruct and inspire students of the dance.

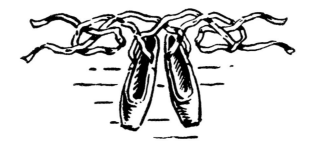

Stephanie Batt

Selection of Ballet Programme covers 1952-1958

THE BALLET RAMBERT

GAIETY THEATRE

COMMENCING JUNE 9th, 1958

FOR ONE WEEK ONLY

PRIOR TO SADLERS WELLS AND CONTINENTAL TOUR

WESTERN THEATRE BALLET

Patron : **MOIRA SHEARER**

Artistic Directors :

ELIZABETH WEST and PETER DARRELL

mimed this Group in 1958

PRICES

Dress Circle	Parterre	Grand Circle
10/-	7/6	6/- & 4/-

Special Prices for Dancing School Parties

and also unfortunately in 1960

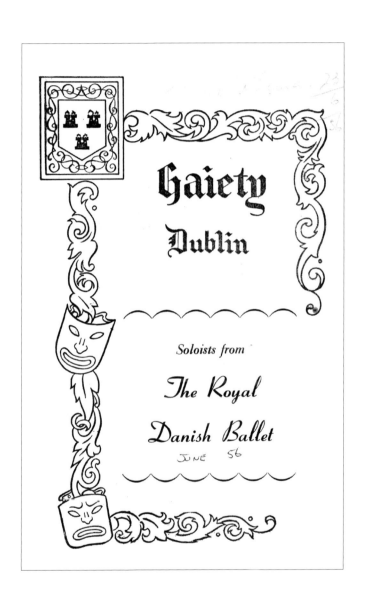

Gaiety

Dublin

Soloists from

The Royal

Danish Ballet

JUNE 56

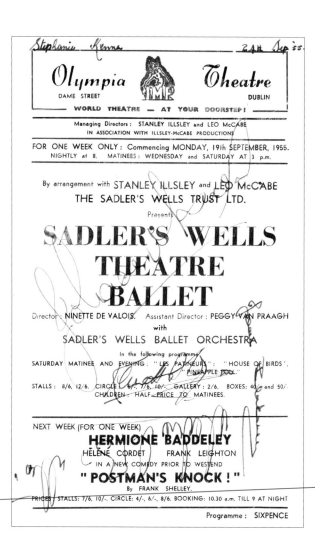

Stephanie Kenna   *24th Sep 55.*

Olympia Theatre
DAME STREET   DUBLIN

— WORLD THEATRE — AT YOUR DOORSTEP!

Managing Directors : STANLEY ILLSLEY and LEO McCABE
IN ASSOCIATION WITH ILLSLEY-McCABE PRODUCTIONS

FOR ONE WEEK ONLY : Commencing MONDAY, 19th SEPTEMBER, 1955.
NIGHTLY at 8.   MATINEES : WEDNESDAY and SATURDAY AT 3 p.m.

By arrangement with STANLEY ILLSLEY and LEO McCABE
THE SADLER'S WELLS TRUST LTD.

Presents

SADLER'S WELLS
THEATRE
BALLET

Director : NINETTE DE VALOIS.   Assistant Director : PEGGY VAN PRAAGH

with

SADLER'S WELLS BALLET ORCHESTRA

In the following programme

SATURDAY MATINEE AND EVENING : " LES PATINEURS " : " HOUSE OF BIRDS ",
" PINEAPPLE POLL."

STALLS : 8/6, 12/6. CIRCLE : 6/-, 7/6, 10/-. GALLERY : 2/6. BOXES : 40/- and 50/-.
CHILDREN : HALF PRICE TO MATINEES.

NEXT WEEK (FOR ONE WEEK)

HERMIONE BADDELEY
HÉLÈNE CORDET   FRANK LEIGHTON
IN A NEW COMEDY PRIOR TO WESTEND

"POSTMAN'S KNOCK!"
By FRANK SHELLEY.

PRICES : STALLS: 7/6, 10/-. CIRCLE: 4/-, 6/-, 8/6. BOOKING: 10.30 a.m. TILL 9 AT NIGHT

Programme : SIXPENCE

Stephanie Renne

Stephanie Renne 1952.
June 18th

Gaiety DUBLIN

PROGRAMME

Commencing
MONDAY, 2nd JUNE, 1952, for THREE WEEKS

Evenings at 7.30 p.m.
Matinees : Wednesday and Saturday at 2.30 p.m.

CHOREOGRAPHIC PRODUCTIONS LIMITED
Present under the Direction of
MONA INGLESBY

INTERNATIONAL BALLET

MONA INGLESBY

HELENE ARMFELT	SOPHIA TRANT
ALGERANOFF	ENA BAGULEY
DENYS PALMER	MALCOLM HUGHES
JOYCE GEARING	DAVID LUSBY
JOHN HEALY	HERIDA MAY
JEANETTE MINTY	ERROL ADDISON
DOROTHY WALKER	VLADIMIR
MARGARET DREW	KALICHEVSKY
CLAUDIE	MYRA KIDD
ALGERANOVA	ANTHONY WALLIS
ERNEST HEWITT	JUNE SUMMERS
YAT MALMGREN	CHARLES LEY
BRIDGET KELLY	ROBERT BLAKE

INTERNATIONAL BALLET ORCHESTRA
Conductors : JAMES WALKER, ANTHONY BAINES
During the playing of the Overture silence is requested

THE BALLET RAMBERT

Stephanie Kennes.   *Sat. 19th Feb. 1955.*

Olympia Theatre

DAME STREET   DUBLIN

WORLD THEATRE —— AT YOUR DOORSTEP!

Managing Directors: STANLEY ILLSLEY and LEO McCABE

IN ASSOCIATION WITH ILLSLEY-McCABE PRODUCTIONS

FINAL WEEK: COMMENCING MONDAY, 14th FEBRUARY, 1955.
NIGHTLY AT 8 p.m.   MATINEE: SATURDAY AT 3 p.m.

STANLEY ILLSLEY **and** LEO McCABE
present

LES ETOILES DES

BALLETS *de* FRANCE
de JANINE CHARRAT

JANINE CHARRAT   HELENE TRAILINE
JEAN BERNARD LEMOINE
RICHARD ADAMA   XENIA PALLEY

GUEST STAR
MILORAD MISKOVITCH

CLAIRE SOMBERT
MILKO SPARENBLOK

Administrator: ALBERT SARFATI.
Conductor of Orchestra: DANIEL STIRN.
Pianiste: JACQUELINE EMERY.

NEXT WEEK Illsley-McCabe announce FOR ONE WEEK
FIRST IRISH PRODUCTION OF THE *PLAY* OF

" JOHNNY BELINDA "
with SORREL CARSON

STAR OF THE PARIS, MILAN AND ROME PRODUCTIONS

POPULAR PRICES: BOOKING UP TO 9 p.m. NIGHTLY.

Programme: SIXPENCE.

Immediately following Sensational Christma

For TWO Weeks ONLY, Commencin

LONDON'S

BAL

GAIETY
THEATRE
DUBLIN

Resident Manager : Phil O'Kelly

Evenings at 8.0 p.m.   Matinees : Wednesdays and Saturdays at 2.30 p.m.

A Festival Ballet programme cover